ANNA POCIASK

The Pilgrimage Of Divorce

AN AWAKENING TO RESTORATION

*To my precious babies, Abigail and Jaden.
Thank you for cheering mommy on even when you
did not understand why mama was crying at the oddest
moments, hugging me when you saw me on my knees in my
bedroom, and being strong through such a confusing time.
You two are my life. I love you both dearly. And I will always
eat you up like a buttercup.*

Contents

1. Your Voyage Starts Here
2. Return to Your First Love
3. Wait and Be Still
4. When my Pilgrimage was Awoken
5. Drop Your Bags: It is Go Time
6. Holy Surrender
7. Brokenness Brings you to your Calling
8. Rest in His Pursuit
9. Roar of Deception: Loneliness
10. He strips us to Heal our Wounds
11. God makes a home for the Lonely
12. Look up and Get Lost in His Presence
13. An Isolated Anger
14. Vulnerable: The Foxes are on the Prowl
15. Lock all the Doors: Strongholds
16. Identify and Admit Those Dragons
17. Identity
18. Honest Wanderer
19. Branded: By the Big Daddy in Heaven
20. Confidence: Your Greatest Weapon
21. Wait: Don't Settle
22. Purity
23. Forgive Yourself
24. Children: They Need You
25. Faith
26. Hope: Rest
27. Embrace His Love
28. Thankful Heart

The Pilgrimage of Divorce

AN AWAKENING TO RESTORATION

To the lonely and vulnerable this is my prayer as you open these pages:

That your love will flourish and that you will not only love much but well. Learn to love appropriately. You need to use your head and test your feelings so that your love is sincere and intelligent, not sentimental gush. Live a lover's life, circumspect and exemplary, a life Jesus will be proud of: bountiful in fruits from the soul, making Jesus Christ attractive to all, getting everyone involved in the glory and praise of God. (Philippians 1:9-11)

God brings us to a place of desperate hunger on purpose; to test our hearts and reveal where we need Him most. Courage will come with humility. Admitting our weaknesses will make us stronger—running from our temptations will bring lasting satisfaction. It takes a humble person to admit where they are weak and a courageous person to run from temptation.

This is about a pilgrimage, but ultimately about the glory the Lord deserves, walking in blind obedience, waiting for the Lord to renew my strength, breaking my will, and falling madly in love with my first love—my King, my Creator, my Sustainer, my Comforter, and my Husband.

Your Voyage Starts Today

Are you fed up being angry because you are angry and exhausted from being tired? And are you ready to stop being stubborn and giving into every quick fix to ease your pain? Before you step on board are you seeking an easy feel good, self-help book? If so, when ready your story of restoration will be waiting on the other side of the horizon. It is not until you admit your entanglements, hang-ups, quick fixes, and addictions that stemmed from your divorce you'll be ready to step on ship to freedom. I am not here to patch your wounds, but to straight up get to the core of the issue. You have seen how far your "self-help" has gotten you. I want to show you that even before our divorce we had strongholds lurking around; but they probably did not latch on and pull you down until you were most vulnerable and weak; after the trauma of your divorce. I want to lead you to a safe place of regaining trust.
Self-help has us rely on ourselves, not the One who can truly mend what needs to be restored. Jesus wants to bind up our wounds and heal us, not fill our minds with some puffed up knowledge that still leaves you feeling empty and parched.

Have you finally admitted you are a mess and are fed up with running around wasting your time on alcohol, men, cheap romantic novels, clothes, and binge eating?

You will not find a 10 steps to recovery here. As I know not one pilgrimage will be the same, so why would I dare put you in a box and lead you to go by steps, rather lead you to search **your pain**, strongholds, and how to truly rely on the One that has all the answers. You are the only one that truly knows the steps you are ready to take. There are many days ahead of you that will encounter moments of confident leaps; but pace yourself, this is not race; **this is your story of regaining something that was stolen into a magnificent testimony of a sweeter gift in exchange.**

Pilgrim—you can either choose to make this voyage heavy or light. Drop any baggage that is weighing you down, take a deep breath and walk without guilt, shame, worry, and fear. As you journey to the other side of freedom and confidence along you are allowed to add to your bag; courage, trust, hope, joy, and thankfulness! ☺ Pilgrims cast their eyes on the prize ahead; never looking back. You are journeying from a city of destruction to a city of freedom and hope. No obstacle comes without a reward. Your reward will be better than anything this world can offer-- Joy, thankfulness, peace, and confidence are waiting to be yours.

Ummmm Anna, wait just a minute; you have no clue what hell I have been through!! You are absolutely correct, I do not, but I do hope to hear how you let the Lord transform you from the inside out. And I do know you are reading thus far because you are seeking hope from the One that is in the business of healing. So are you wondering how this applies to all the pain you are facing after your spouse just left you? I will tell you a little secret. This is NOT about him anymore, this is all about YOU. You are going to have to trust me. Divorce gets messy really quick and I am not naïve that when we are lonely, shattered, and feeling unloveable we take matters into our own hands. Then the next thing we know we begin telling ourselves we are "healthy" when ultimately we are bored and not patient enough to heal.

Whatever expectation and experience you want for your life this instant, just go ahead and throw it out the window. No for real. I am serious. Do something for me right now. If you do not have an empty journal in your home, go get you one right now. I will be presenting a lot of questions not just for you to think about, but to answer and truly reflect on what God is doing with your weary soul. Jesus is in the business of showering us with wowzer revelations; which means He wants to take us to the root of our pain. **Suffering and pain is everyone's destiny to a whole new life of blissful rejoicing.** I think we are champions of having anointed amnesia; so do not forget to stop and smell the rich soil of your unique story. A smell can take me back years to the exact spot I was standing and envisioning. **Breathe in the sorrowful days so you never forget where God is going to lead you to a life of confidence.**

You need a big bold title for this journal: MY PILGRIMAGE AWAITS. ONWARD! #thepilgrimageofdivorce

Return to Your First Love

**WARNING—What I am about to say may bring knots to your stomach, gritting of your teeth, possible holy swearing at me, or maybe JUST maybe a surrendering to YOUR will.

I ask you to search your heart on giving it to the One who fashioned it **for one whole year**. Go ahead, read that line again. Yes-a whole year of **pure** dedication to letting your First Love pursue you and teach you what genuine love looks, feels, and tastes like. I respect this is ultimately between you and God; but to save you some heartache I will give you the ending—**He will win and not give up His ultimate purpose for your life.** When He intricately designed your heart He knew there was going to be scars to come, oozing wounds, and unbelievable heartache. So, here you are, seeking for a cure, a word to bring hope, a touch of relief that all will be well with your soul. I am here to tell you there is One that *"wants you all for Himself"* (2 Cor. 6:15) And not only is He the One waiting for you to cry and ask for His healing hand to forgive whoever you need to forgive; whether that be yourself or your x-spouse, more than likely both. He will not stop there sweet soul; when He sees your focus and dedication to walk with faith again, you will hear with a strong voice as He told the paraplegic in Mark 2...."Get up, Pick up your stretcher and go home." God does not want you to have a crippled heart any longer. **But pay close attention because this pain you carry will one day turn into your story of redemption.**

When we are in our most desperate and sorrowful times is when we are most in tune with our weaknesses. How? Because we act on them, and if you have not, you have tortured your mind with thoughts of defeat. And in these weaknesses I want you to find as I have; His grace is sufficient. And in these what seems to be lonely days I want you to find there are hidden miracles waiting to be revealed. This pain you're experiencing is part of your journey to becoming a new you, a stronger you, a brave you, a confident you, a wise you, a blessed you, and a faithful you. I know you are hurting. I know you want to speed through this book in hopes to be free on your way to joyous living, but be patient with your pilgrimage. Do not ever doubt the Lord is drawing you near.

WAIT AND BE STILL

Waiting is the transformation of something to blossom. Waiting may seem stagnant; but rest assured because one day you will look back and see the beauty that was unfolding all along. Whether we acknowledge it or not, all of us have something in common with the theme in our life; **waiting**. Truth be told we are professionals at being impatient and not waiting. Have you ever wondered where this stir of MORE came from? Go dive into Romans 8:22-23 and see what The Spirit reveals to you during this time of waiting.

> *"For we know that the whole creation has been groaning together in the pains of childbirth until now. 23 And not only the creation, but we ourselves, who have the firstfruits of the Spirit, groan inwardly as we wait eagerly for adoption as sons, the redemption of our bodies."*

The odd creatures that we are have a lot of commonality, however the difference comes in how we respond, react, and receive this gift of grace. The destiny God had paved for us all along. **We are the only one that gets in the way of believing we are too stained for God to make a new avenue for our lives.** I know you feel as if the rug was just pulled from underneath your feet and when you fell on your ass everyone was staring at you, talking about you, whispers all around saying how did she not see that was coming. You feel humiliated, bruised up, and feel like a complete failure for not being more alert. Guess what—this is not about the spouse that left you, this is not about what other people are saying about you, this is about a pilgrim warrior that is placing her feet on new territory with confidence!

Will you wait on whatever the Lord asks of you, move to the side and let Him truly lead you? This is your pilgrimage; guard it well, tend it often, allow it to blossom, and you will find yourself able to trust once again.

When My Pilgrimage Was Awoken

July 27, 2014

*Keep in mind as of October 2013 is when my x-husband and I became separated.

Darkness is all around me, my bed is cold and lonely as there is no more warmth radiating and deep snores keeping me company. I am a freaking mess—dark thoughts are taking over every waking moment of my being. I am losing control of all areas of my life and running thin on waiting for my husband to return. One more glance to see if it was almost morning, but the clock showed it was only midnight.

As we all know sin creeps in nice and slow; warming us up to the thought of taking a bite toward a better life. However there was no life being received rather the opposite of a slow strangle of being suffocated.

Enough was enough, no matter which way I situated my pillow, positioned myself perfectly on my belly with securing pillows all around me, sleeping was not going to take place until I took down my walls and got up to pray. I walked straight to my children's rooms, got on my knees and began weeping. The tears rolled down my cheeks where then the salty taste of bitterness touched my lips and this is when I began to plead. Lord protect their hearts and minds and bring peace over their souls. No matter how diligent I am in nurturing them, loving them, talking openly about our home situation, in all reality this is not what God wants for families. My family may not appear to be as picturesque as we use to be, but this is my family now.

We may be one less piece to our once puzzle; but I choose to let God fill in the gaps and pick up the broken pieces with His faithfulness.

The root of the distraction came from wanting to be desired, pursued, and adored. I was letting it eat away at my soul rather fighting for delight in the Lord. Once I got up and sought His affections, He gave me rest. A chipping away of my selfish wants was in the works and hands of the ultimate crafter and refiner. When I woke a new sense of purpose came over my body; His peace and direction were overshadowing any anxious thought and numb feeling. **Our dreams are originally His calling on our life that in the end keeps us accountable from lures of the world.**

When we choose to believe we are alone we choose to do desperate actions.
For example: A few weeks ago I received an "innocent" message on Facebook from another single individual. I was flattered and found myself wanting to latch on quickly to his pursuit. **Flattery leads us to a road of compromise when vulnerable.**

The conviction of the Spirit was so thick I could not eat, and began losing way too much weight. The knots in my stomach were so tight I was in a constant state of nausea. I was too stubborn and selfish to realize The Spirit was giving me answers before I was even asking for them. The Lord was no where close being done with me; he only used that one man to wake me up and continue the pursuit of His love. When I realized I was putting this male before God, all satisfaction for God left me. I wanted to fill my void of loneliness, guilt, and grief as quickly as possible. There was absolutely no peace in this little fling. Ultimately, I was alone and wanted to feel pursued, when all along God was in the works of His calling on my life. **Simply put, desperate and solo times make way for a clouded vision.** Because in just those two short weeks my mind raced with thoughts of a new future with a man I barely even knew. It turned into a shamble of disappointment very quickly. Which lead me to a snapping point. This was the last thing that needed to happen and God was not done with me yet. Quite frankly, He was just getting started and was loud and clear there was **much** that needed chiseled away in my soul.

"Do not worship any other god, for the Lord, whose name is Jealous, is a jealous God." Exodus 34:14

July 28, 2014 I began writing the first words of this book, and as my son held onto me from behind it was as if God was reminding me, I will hold you the whole way, and be here directing your words. *"Draw near to me, and I will draw near to you."* James 4:8

On this day the Lord challenged me to a commitment of not seeking any romantic relationship with a man, nor even flirt with the idea of pursuing a relationship.

God was saying WAIT and REST as I wanted to do things my way and be the furthest away from being still. At the time I did not realize I feared man over God; because rather completely trusting and obeying I feared Id miss an opportunity but in hindsight I could have missed Gods calling. But He does not give a vision without a purpose. His purpose was to reveal to me my lack of self-control and lack of trust in Him.

After the long year of lessons I now am ready to receive the desires that captivate my heart. I now fear Him and what pleases Him. I keep myself out of traps that could cause unnecessary heartache.

What has awoken your pilgrimage?

Will you promise me to take it slow when you read, dig into the scriptures, reflect on what God wants to teach you, and seek an understanding of this pain you are bearing is for a purpose. My hero of the faith will always be Elisabeth Elliot and she once said and knows by experience—"*suffering is never for nothing.*" Find great courage that your heartache assures that your soul has life. You are here to be reminded "pain is no evil, unless it conquers us." Says Charles Kingsley. I pray you find much encouragement through my journey of regaining who I am in Christ during my weakest moments. It is my passion to hear miracle stories of broken sinners clinging to the hope and steadfast love of our Savior and Creator. I want to hear how you let God carry you every step of the way. This is no quick journey. It takes much healing; genuine get down into the infected wound healing; no band-aids allowed here.

Your pilgrimage awaits! Onward toward tasting and seeing what God wants to free you from.

Drop Your Bags...It is Go Time

Are you ready to dive into the heavy sin that has entangled you from walking in freedom?

There are no hidden agendas here; just one sinner pouring her struggles out on paper to reveal Gods hope to other broken individuals seeking His grace and healing. Maybe you were unfaithful in your marriage, now separated or divorced and want nothing more than restoration in your relationship with the Lord. Whether you were left or you left, you are here searching for healing and I am so proud of you for taking this step! You are a beautiful masterpiece with a lifetime ahead of you that gets to make things right in your heart. This is a place where I want you to know me, feel like we are sitting down over a cup of coffee chatting about real life. If we see one another don't be shy, because I am a hugger and want to look into your eyes and tell you how beautiful you are.

Are you ready to commit to whatever the Lord is telling you to let go of? When you are ready to wait and hold off on the worlds best, in place for Gods best, then turn the page and welcome yourself to a ride toward freedom. Dive into my journey of hopeful solitude, stubborn obedience, and the closest relationship I've ever experienced with Jesus Christ. To His name be the glory!

Holy Surrender

"May the Lord direct your hearts to the love of God and to the steadfastness of Christ"
2 Thessalonians 3:5

Silence out the noise. Shut out the distracting world. Close the door behind you. Get on your knees. And begin a new routine. This practice will turn into your most prized possession. Welcome the Holy Spirit. Make it a safe dwelling place. And find yourself so immersed in His Presence you will never want to leave your sacred meeting place. There is no set agenda or formula when it comes to laying your burdens down, shedding your tears, or simply just giving thanks. It took me after my year commitment to close my closet door in holy surrender; as His Word is what I feast on for strength, confidence, and purpose. I pray you will find yourself so hungry for His presence nothing of this world will come close to snaring you. He is the Prince of Wholeness, a gift given to us to unwrap daily. He never grows old but only gets sweeter each time you embrace His Presence.

Write these six statements down in your journal, put them up in your closet or wherever your prayer chamber will be. This is your sacred place where the Holy Spirit will sense your vigorous commitment. (or purchase a print in my shop online)

RELEASE your heart to the One that fashioned it perfectly for a purpose that will absolutely blow your mind.
RAISE your arms in faithful surrender.
REPENT and drop your chains to walk in freedom.
RELISH in His sweet and satisfying presence.
RENEW your spirit in the knowledge of His holy Word.

RESPOND to His voice.

Being sensitive has probably become a familiar friend of yours. Why not give that sensitivity to the Lords leading in your life?

I want you to describe the relationship you have with the Lord in this season of your life right now. And if you are thinking--- what relationship? Just be real, write it down. Today will look way different than a year from now.

i LEAN ON THE LORD NOW MORE THAN i EVER HAVE. i JUST HAVE A HARD TIME PRAYING & HEARING FROM THE SPIRIT.

Where would you like to see yourself in a year emotionally, spiritually, intellectually, and even physically?

SPIRITUALLY - LEADING OTHERS GOING THROUGH THIS.

INTELLECTUALLY - ALMOST DONE WITH MY DEGREE.

PHYSICALLY - WELL WITH A GOOD IMMUNE SYSTEM. HEALTHY.

EMOTIONALLY - HEALED FROM MY BROKEN HEART, TRULY FORGIVEN JORDAN & HIS FAMILY. A PEACE LIKE NO OTHER SUCH JOY

Brokenness Brings You To Your Calling

Are you willing to give up something that is hindering your love relationship with the One that fashioned your heart and brought you into this world for purpose?

YES — THAT SOMETHING WAS JORDAN. I PUT HIM ABOVE ALL ELSE. HE'S NOT MY RESCUER THE LORD IS.

My ring finger feels so exposed and naked. Many years my wedding finger was embellished by a symbol that represented I was taken and spoken for. And now a sense of panic comes over me when the two fingers that once grazed next to that symbol of commitment is not there. But, quickly I am reminded it is not because I forgot to put it on, but that it is no longer wanted to be there. Then I have to face the reminder all over again that this symbol is no longer desired by the one that placed it there so proudly with such high hopes and dreams. My finger does feel a little lighter and disconnected from the vein that streams straight to my heart. Our senses are in tune with our soul, that symbol of love was daily put on by choice from a habitual love. It makes sense our heart will need time to heal from that sense of touch that swelled everytime our heart beat through the vein that pumped back and forth to our symbol of love. A part of our identity was stripped away when we last took off our ring and never slipped it back on.

==No matter what our marital status states today, our identity in Christ will never be taken away from us. Your identity has been shaken, but not destroyed.== Just watch and see your identity slowly shift to an awakening that all along was there but misplaced with an earthly clothing that had your affection before the Lord. Let us return to our first love.

No calling will come without struggling and no struggling comes without a purpose.

Rest in His Pursuit

"But then I will win her back once again. I will lead her into the desert and speak tenderly to her there." Hosea 2:14

You ARE taken.
The Lord is smitten by who you are this day.
You do not have to concern yourself with being disappointed with your relationship with Him.
He will stay true to His pursuit of your heart.
He will only speak truth to you.
He will listen to you with open arms.
He will respond to you with wisdom and dedication.
He will protect you from the darkness of this world.
He will go before you.
He will never leave you.

In times of desperation, may we not fall prey to being destroyed by the woos of this world. Instead may we ask favor of The Lord to continue making us desperate for Him, staying comfortable entices us to wander away and stop feeling the need for a Savior.

*"The Bridegroom left on a journey just before the wedding and the Bride cannot act as if things are normal. If she loves him, she will **ache** for his return."* pg 86 (A Hunger for God)
And here I am today learning all over again that we all have an area we continually fall back into, however we have a God that knows our struggles even better than we can comprehend. **And since He is devoted to His sheep He will bring us back to the same place over and over again until we are entirely His.** He wants us to ache for Him as He aches

for our devotion. The only way we will stop letting the wolves deceive us into the darkness of the night is when we avoid the snares of temptation. He wants you to walk in freedom. He wants you to let Him protect you from future and present harm. Come and return back to His pasture of unlimited feasts through the knowledge of His Word.

All the things of this life are rubbish compared to the way He loves us. You have been wounded and need to be reminded there is One God that has His eyes on you solely. When you are feeling alone, not cherished or adored remember there is One that is loving you like no one else is capable of loving.

His love is always loyal.
His love will always be faithful.
His love is committed to us.
His love is devoted to never letting us go.
His love is committed to protect you and go before you.
His love is devoted to pursuing you.
His love is reliable.
His love is determined to not let you stray.
His love is single-mindedly focused on YOU.

Remember this is YOUR pilgrimage. Would you rather go round and round in circles leading you back to your original pains? Or rather move toward freedom?

The Lord gives us the desires of our hearts, and designed us to complete man. God knew when Adam needed Eve to complete him. God lead them together and brought them face to face in Gods perfect timing. God had much work for Adam to do before He saw fit for them to come together as a team. Just as

God is shaping, mending, and luring you He is ultimately preparing you to love as He loves you.

Do you find yourself distracted often with thoughts of some man to share your life with? I cannot give you a timeframe of when God will be done binding up your wounds to release you into the world of companionship again. If you know without a doubt the Lord has created you to bring good to another man then do not rush it. It is in our DNA and fashion to want to supply strength in areas a man may not be capable of handling on his own. And not a strength that comes over him, but one that walks alongside him and compliments him.

I want you to look at Genesis 2:18 from a different angle... *"Then the Lord God said, "It is not good that the man should be alone; I will **make** him a helper fit for him."* Before we get all antsy and ready to be on the prowl again lets consider the perfecting that is taking place in your soul right now. Alright so we already know it is not good for man to be alone, but do we know that God is MAKING you perfectly for him? I love taking one word from a sentence and dissecting it to go deeper and challenge me intellectually and spiritually. When I looked up the word "make" many encouraging words popped up that I think will give you much motivation to let God do what He is best at doing—shaping us into His Son. God is a man of His word and He will perfect you into a helper if you are willing to let Him.

I will FORM him a helper...
I will PUT TOGETHER him a helper...
I will FASHION him a helper...
I will PREPARE him a helper...
I really like this one.... I will BREW him a helper. (We will smell so inviting he wont know what hit him. When Adam

awoke from his deep sleep the *brew* of Eve knocked him silly) ☺

 I will DELIVER him a helper...
 I will SELECT him a helper...

We must wait for God to do His perfecting, not take the reigns and mess it all up by "making" it happen. We as women are good at manipulating, controlling, and making sure our needs get met. This is a time of learning to let God pursue you, adore you, douse you in gifts, and give you your confidence back in a new and fresh way.

What is luring you into the traps of desiring mans attention over Gods affection?

What step of faith are you willing to take today?

Roar of Deception: Loneliness

"Take no part in the unfruitful works of darkness, but instead expose them." (Ephesians 5:11)

The roar of temptation deceives us into the arms of death. It is said not to be afraid of where the roar is coming from, but where the roar is making you run to out of fear. I am not certain running to the roar would be anywhere safe either, but the ploy the lion makes the vulnerable prey believe is to run from the loud roar, when in reality it is forcing the prey to run right to the lion waiting on the other end to destroy you.

Loneliness has roared loud so many times I ended up in the arms of a man or a bottle of too many to sound out the roar, but in the end was lead to believe if I ran from the roar I would feel secure when I did not hear nor feel the pain of loneliness anymore. God guaranteed suffering for the Christian but He never encouraged us to escape it. It's in these moments of deceptive roars we must listen to the real King of Roars. It is in moments like these your fear will reveal whom your trust is in.

What is the roar that is striking fear up and down your spine, puts knots in your stomach, or brings you to a sobbing mess of tears?

I want you to call it out now in the name of Jesus. And everytime the roar of loneliness, doubt, worry, or whatever is deceiving you---remember this. We have to conquer these tests to become a conqueror. So rather beating yourself up one more time for running to get away from the roar you get to proclaim from the rooftops the test that turned into your biggest testimony! God chooses the weak and humble. He knows in your weakness you will turn to Him for strength. Your weak moments do not define you. You will be defined by how you did not let your weaknesses defeat you!

He Strips us To Heal Our Wounds

Divorce hurts. No matter how much we cling to the hope of Jesus and people tell you to press on and get in the Word, the pain resurfaces when we least expect it. The more in tune you get with your pain the more aware you will be with how the Lord is stripping band-aids off of you to get to the deeper wound. I can tell when I give up one *avoidance of pain—*I fill it with something else. And I picked up way too much alcohol this week, and deep down I do not desire to be drunk. But, I truthfully can say I drink to numb pain away.
He strips me to heal me. Seems like a hard concept to understand, until you are going through it. He strips us of the things that do not belong.

"He heals the brokenhearted and binds up their wounds" (Psalm 147:3)

One morning I was weeping in my bed as being lonely attacked me right at my deepest core. It was a late night with friends and my kids celebrating the New Year and I knew I needed to rest and then get in the Word as I have learned the hard way when tired and not fed by scripture I tend to wander down a path of believing lies. But I could not get myself to rest, rather I called a dear friend and just wept over the phone with her. Even as I write right now I am being attacked with heavy feelings of being alone, it is almost putting me to a point of numbness where I cant move.
I am not going to let this defeat me. Here are the lies that maybe you can relate with—are you familiar with any of these?

You're all alone and nobody wants to be with you.
You ruined your marriage and now you sit in a quiet home with nobody to share life with.
You only know how to ruin relationships.
Regret is becoming your good friend.

So yea I sit here on my bed feeling completely broken, which I know deep down this is right where God wants me. Completely relying on Him for strength. But this pain, it feels too broken and ripped to be complete again. But, have I ever truly believed in the Prince of Wholeness? It is quite clear I have chosen to be a wandering soul running after what feels good, abusing grace. Is this part of the healing? Is this the message you have been trying to tell me, Lord? To admit I am broken, and **pain is assurance my soul is alive.**

After all the running around, drinking myself to sleep, empty conversations to fill voids of pain, life catches up to you eventually. Because we were created for so much more! The end result I have found myself in is being alone; alone right where God wants me, alone with Him. False happiness I do not want you any longer. True healing to my deepest wounds, my soul cries out for. One day at a time. And rather believing the lie of nobody wants me, I will redirect that thought with God is protecting me. To every no, He has a bigger yes. And this yes will come when we realize every no He protected us from we know longer will find satisfaction from. He wants to heal me and prepare my heart so one day when I marry again I will be a woman that is able to live by these words in Isaiah 43... *"forget about what's happened; don't keep going over old history. Be alert. Be present. I'm about to do something brand-new. It's bursting out! Don't you see it? There it is! I'm making a road through the desert, rivers in the badlands."*

And as I have made many unwise choices in times of desperation while most vulnerable I am breathing in this quote from Oswald Chambers.... *"Leave the broken, irreversible past in God's hands, and step out into the invincible future with Him."*

Genuine brokenness comes with the breaking of your will. When we surrender to our will it is similar to a break-up because we give up all the things we thought we needed to keep pressing on to obedience.

Brokenness wakes us up to the beauty of our worth. Once you understand the precious presence of the Spirit wants to dwell within YOU, your pain will soon turn into laughter, thankfulness and confidence.

Brokenness draws us to the Cross. Brokenness brings us to a life of humility and total surrender. When broken you taste the richness of His love. Stay broken and stay desperate for His love.

God makes a home for the lonely (Psalm 68:6)

This home the psalmist speaks of is the arms of His presence. This home is letting go of all your burdens and letting Him carry them for us. As treacherous it is to imagine Jesus carrying that wooden cross to Calvary, He did it for this sole purpose. So we would not be alone in our moments of weakness, sorrow, and aching hearts. It's in our moments of solitude we hear Him the loudest. **This home of loneliness is Gods glory in disguise**. Let Him have it, let Him have your whole being. This home is a safe place to rest our weary souls. This lonely place is not unaccompanied at all, rather quite the opposite.

As you are shedding tears, numb from the pain, angry, exhausted, sick, confused and feel like life is spinning out of control. You ARE still moving forward. Life does not standstill. It only can get better. It can only move onward. This is your pilgrimage—don't waste it.

Look Up and Get Lost in His Presence

*"Being confident of this, that he who began a good work in you will **carry** it on to **completion** until the day of Christ Jesus." (Phil. 1:6) NIV*

Defense mechanisms suck, as when facing pain and no emotion filter's out due to the numbing pain of denial. We will only find pure joy in our hearts once we let God be our center and focus. Man can NEVER fulfill us completely if outside the will of God. Our hearts were fashioned to relish a complete joy, not the deceitful temporary lures of the world, which we are so easily swayed to settle for. I refuse to settle. I refuse to give myself away too quickly for the return of a good feeling. I refuse to throw my hands up and give into pleasure when my body oh so craves it.

As I sit here and write I see an empty chair across the table, but in my heart I now imagine that seat being reserved for Jesus. Over this year in a half that chair has slowly faded from my vision, as when I stop and truly let myself look over at the emptiness it resembles, memories flood my heart and vision that bring pain. However today I feel the pull to look there with courage and confidence. I cannot help but smile each time I flicker my eyes over there to an empty chair with so much beauty. Because I know this chair is not empty. I feel the presence of the spirit gazing back at me as my eyes are filling with tears. I feel so beautiful and desired at this very moment. He has been there all along—waiting for me to blush at His pursuit of my heart. I have not felt this beautiful in a long time. He has not taken His eyes off of me once. He is enthralled to be acknowledged. How long has He waited for me to look up and get lost into His presence? Will you look up, invite Him into your room and make it a beautiful dwelling place for Him?

Many days I have to fight the lies of feeling unlovable. But today as I cannot keep my eyes off this chair I feel Jesus reaching over for my hand to assure me I am loveable, beautiful, clean, and desirable. He wants to have your heart in His hands to protect it, nourish it, cleanse it, and pump it with

His pursuit. As I stand up from the seat, He does not remain there. He gets up and walks alongside me.

This was a spark of confidence that flared in the midst of sorrow, insecurity, and doubt in whom I was as an individual. Even though I share of this beautiful reminder from the Lord, I still had much breaking and relying to do on God. Its moments like these that kept me moving onward.

An Isolated Anger

I'm angry my marriage ended
I'm angry I'm alone
I'm angry any man I meet does not want anything to do with God
I'm angry because I want to be pursued
I'm angry because I wake every 2 hours in the night.
I'm angry because I'm angry
I'm angry because I am really hungry but right when I walk in the door alone the desire to eat goes away.

And now what—the ugly dragon that brings out the irritable you is lurking around again. You thought anger was an old friend that had been dealt with, sealed with a kiss, and said syronara to. But in all reality these stages of grief we battle through do not ever completely go away. They are going to flare up in a different way; and as time passes they will feel like an old friend you are familiar with but dance around the room trying to not make eye contact, trying to hide behind the potato bar at the class reunion; stuffing your face with all that gooey goodness of cheese, butter, and sour cream. And right at that instant, you look up, mouth full, not able to say a word. The whole room goes quiet, and there you stand face to face with this ugly old emotion. Let's be honest; this ugly emotion needs to go. It is not healthy for your blood pressure or attractive to anyone around you. I understand there is a time and place to let out your aggrevation, believe me I did and I so wish I could go back and respond differently. If this gives you a little relief to understand why you're angry I will share it with you, but you have to promise me you will toss anger out. Anger is a natural emotion that was given to us, but it is our choice to manage it and control it. Anger flares up when we have lost control; hence your divorce may not have been on your decision and you lost complete control on the choice that was made. Anger also flares up when your body is just plain tired of crying; it moves into a stage of rage because you feel your in control now rather the tears controlling you. Just a few things to ponder on, but it is up to you how you want to respond and engage. I am praying you choose to admit your angry and express why you are angry. It will help if you write down why you are angry rather yelling at the one you are angry with.

What will you do with it now?

Will you keep stuffing yourself with food, sex, alcohol, romantic novels, or buying new clothes to sound out the One that is trying to get a clear message across to you?

As I was sharing my heart with my mom she then asked me; why do you not want to be alone with yourself? At that very moment I was not able to answer that question. I did not even realize the thought of struggling with being alone with myself.

But then I heard the painful lie, *"if I am alone then deep down my soul believes nobody wants me."*

HOWEVER.....

A warrior **trusts** the unseen but is not naive.
A warrior does not take her eye off the end prize which is a destined life of **freedom**.
Rest in your loneliness and **be still** so He can mend you.

The more FULL you are of thankfulness and joyfulness the easier it will be to walk in contentment. When content you are not searching for more than what's already been given to you to nurture. Nourish what has been given to you this day and watch it grow into your greatest gift. Thankfulness is attractive.

Before you can walk in confidence you need to be reminded who you are. But even before that you need to be aware of the strongholds that are "holding" you back from freedom.

You are not JUST passing through you are GETTING to pass through.

Vulnerable: The Foxes are on the Prowl

Attraction comes with being still. Cast out your thoughts of worry. That only attracts the enemy to steal your joy. Enough has been stolen from you. Now it is time to start journeying toward attracting others to your confidence and humblenss. But first you must identify your distractions.

The ultimate test is presented when these three statements sneak into your vulnerable heart:

I am tired.
I am lonely.
I am bored.

    These are three triggers destined for seeking some sort of satisfaction that deceives your weak soul. **You are wiser than you give yourself credit. What outcome do you want in the end—regret or peace?** We get a choice each day to choose instant gratification or delayed genuine affection. I can bet you are inches away from your phone. The phone has turned into the easiest entanglement to avoid pain or stir up unnecessary pain. I know you want someone to talk to and laugh uncontrollably with. If I could I would look you in the eyes right now and say, you are worth so much more than a quick empty thrill. You are easy prey with an open wound. You are not damaged goods. The quicker you admit that you're susceptible, the easier it will be to just be held in the arms of the One that mends the brokenhearted.

> *Don't excite love, don't stir it up, until the time is ripe— and **you're** ready. Song of Songs 2:7*

Peace is a gift. Never doubt it.

Do you feel like you are the only one on the couch tonight with nothing to do? Well guess what, that was me many a night with a box of Nilla wafers and endless searching on Netflix. I know there are many struggling with this right now and it is okay. Sure it sucks, but a new day will come tomorrow with new blessings.
Will you wait for those new blessings? This is when you have to weigh out the cost. You have to look out for everyone's best interest. Will a call or text benefit anyone? How will you feel tomorrow if you give into this urge that will only last tonight?

"For he satisfies the longing soul, and the hungry soul he fills with good things." (Psalm 107:8) ESV

Vulnerable moments are going to creep in when you least expect it; and before you know it, a so called good thing can turn into a replacement of the satisfaction God wants for you. I know from experience that when my children are with me 24-7, then they leave for their dads I am left to a quiet home of nobody to care for, I become numb and don't know what to do with myself at times. THIS is when I have to choose if I will dedicate my time wisely or shallowly.

"Discipline is the wholehearted yes to the call of God. I know myself called, summoned, addressed, taken possession of, known, acted upon, I have heard the Master. I put myself gladly, fully, and forever at His disposal, and to whatever He says my answer is yes." (Elisabeth Elliot from the book Discipline the Glad Surrender)

I think it is important for me to remind myself and to remind you that even once we get to a place of peace, no more crying ourselves to sleep, overcoming temptations, forgiving, and no longer bitter we are still going to have low days. And rather letting these down days creep in and control us, lets examine our surroundings.

Even once we become content with our circumstances, how often do we examine our hearts? Do not get too comfortable in your contentment; as this is when you are able to see the fog lifted, the shedding of tears diminished and now the light shine on your weaknesses. We are not able to accept our weaknesses and insecurities until we humble ourselves enough to realize the pain we carry in our hearts is as real as a heart attack. But the question we need to ask ourselves is this---what do we want to do with the pain that sneaks up on us in our days of joy and contentment?

I personally believe days of longing and pain will hit us when we least expect it because we became one with another flesh; emotionally, spiritually, and physically. We shared our biggest moments in life with that person. For me mine was marriage, moving to the big Texas land, creating two human beings, birthing them, watching one another cry, shared our deepest secrets, separated, and then divorced. These BIG impactful moments are on both ends of the spectrum of pure joy and pain. And to toss these to wasteland is basically saying to yourself none of those moments were real. Sure it be easy to want to forget all of those beautiful bittersweet days, but they happened, and they have shaped you into who you are. We get to decide if want our mold to crumble, be crushed to the ground, or let God pick each piece up and put you back together. I read a quote today that makes no sense to me.... "one of the hardest things to do in life, is letting go of what you thought was real." And here is why I do not like this quote—to me it is saying that person does not believe the emotion, connection, love, and life they shared was all a big lie. **Any mistake that took place will never cancel out all the breaths that were taken together.** There is freedom in releasing tears even when you get to a place of healing and peace. A couple days ago I should have been celebrating my 10 year anniversary and I knew the day was coming up and felt completely okay. But, when the day approached I began weeping and felt freedom in connecting with these tears. These were not bitter tears but healthy tears. An hour or two passed and I was content with the Lord again, as I knew He was holding me and letting me grieve. It is okay to grieve.

God himself is right alongside to keep you steady and on track until things are all wrapped up by Jesus. 9 God, who got you started in this spiritual adventure, shares with us the life of his Son and our Master Jesus. He will never give up on you. Never forget that. (1 Cor. 1:8-9) The MSG

He will not tolerate a lifestyle that represents a mediocre life. **Your life has been turned upside down to remind you that the same God that brought the cosmos out of chaos will bring loveliness out of your purposeful havoc.** He allows us to stay in a lull of a valley that seems heavy on our soul. As He knows what our soul is weary and fed up of giving away. God is not shallow; He goes to the depth and root of our vulnerable hearts to bring to life the purpose He had for us all along. This pursuit will lead you to a life of longing for the Holy Spirit to invade your soul, mind, and simply every inch of your body. Ask Him to invigorate your soul. Ask for the moon.

"The Spirit, not content to flit around on the surface, dives into the depths of God, and brings out what God planned all along." -1 Corinthians 2:1

Lock all The Doors: Strongholds

When I kept silent about my sin, my body wasted away through my groaning all day long." (NASB— Psalms 32:3)

Alcohol: Hey buddy oh pal, we meet again.

Our flesh only knows how to dull pain in a selfish way, which typically involves a quick fix. And how I know that it only dulls our weary and aching soul is because our "quickies" alleviate for only the time being. The next morning you wake up and nothing has changed; the ache is still there and you wonder how early is too early for another drink. I mean the saying is, it's 5:00 somewhere, right?

Even though my children had no idea I was drinking myself to sleep I made a public confession to them that alcohol would not be welcome in our home anymore. They didn't even know what it was; my son thought it was coke. Even though they are seven and almost five I hope the confession I shared with them will impact their hearts to sway their choices later down the road.

I know there are evenings you don't think you can make it until bedtime with your children. Think of it this way—how much do your children mean to you? I am going to guess you would die for them, work three jobs to make ends meet, and bend over backwards to make sure they have all that they need. I say this in love; you have already lost your spouse, do not lose your children too due to loving the way alcohol deceives you into believing you are okay. Every time you choose to say no to a crutch the stronger and more beautiful you will begin to feel. This is the mom your children want to remember—a strong and vibrant mother that pours endless hours of life into their innocent souls.

"look carefully how you walk".... There were nights I drank so much (when my kids were at their dads) I could barely get up off the couch without stumbling over my own feet. I was not using my time wisely, I was wasting my time away numbing out any sort of feeling that was trying to be on the forefront of my mind and heart. Rather than facing my pain I stirred in more poison to keep me from truly healing. It slowly was turning me into a sloth.

When looking back on any regret I have taken part in, it has involved alcohol. My judgement was wavered and I threw out the window all self-control. When not partaking in alcohol my mind and heart are filled with the Spirit and I am more encouraged to fight temptation with God's word and reaching out to my mom, mentors, and close friends.

But the Lord God called to the man and said to him, "Where are you?" (Genesis 3:9)

Even in our darkest hour God still comes after us and asks us...."where are you?" When all along He knew exactly our hearts intension, where our mind had wandered to forbidden thoughts, and places we had gone that only caused us more pain once the release took place. I am certain you are not satisfied with anything the world has offered from the chief of lies. Am I right?

So, where are you today?

What are you trying to hide from God, your children, friends, and family?

If you are not proud enough to share what you are running to behind closed doors then it more than likely is a stronghold. Is there more conviction than peace?

IF we obey, how many will be blessed? IF we disobey, how many will be affected? IF He asked us today to leave behind our old ways to break the chain of iniquity for our children would that change our motives? How much do we love God? I think we can only answer this honestly....

"If you love me, you will obey what I command" (John 14:15)
Yes Lord. I have sealed up the cracks. We all know where our cracks are to let in a little pleasure if we need it later on a low day.
Where have you left a little opening for a taste of "satisfaction?" Seal it up. Fill in the gaps. Nail it closed with 2x4's. Burn it. Get rid of it, completely.

Pilgrim warrior do not give up and do not lose hope. Don't give into the lies of pleasure that will only last for the night.

And I feel the urge to pray....
Dear sweet Jesus, you have never given up on me, as many times I put myself in darkness, and engaged in selfish pleasure. Forgive me Father for disobeying you. Forgive me

Father for making you turn away as I sinned. As dark and light can not be friends. I choose YOU Father. I choose you....forgive me for justifying my actions..over and over again. But thank-you for delivering me. Thank-you for convicting me. Thank-you for the blessings you want to pour down on me. Thank-you for calling me to You. Thank-you for being enough. In Jesus name—Amen

A gut wrenching decision was made while dealing with much sorrow in my soul. I was able to let the Holy Spirit lead me into the grocery store and not go down the liquor aisle to get my aide for sleep and numbing of pain. I sat in my car and made a conscious decision once it was obvious that if I was in this much turmoil to buy wine or not—it was more than likely the The Spirit telling me to not let it control me. And a still small voice came over me—*you are going to be okay.*
 I keep envisioning in my mind smashing wine bottles around me—watching the glass shatter to the ground. Each piece representing death to me—there was no life in any drop that touched my lips. Alcohol became a crutch to help me sleep—to help pass the time go by when my kids were away—and to help me get loose when I knew deep down I did not really want to give myself away sexually. The alcohol always wavered my beliefs and fogged my hearing from the Spirit.

I cannot believe I am saying this—**but I hate alcohol.**
I hate it because it kept me from feeling pain that needed to be dealt with. It was not until tonight in June of 2015 I truly faced pain without letting alcohol numb it away. I truly feel tonight was a turning point when I heard the Lord say—enough is enough—you do not need that anymore. Relax in my hands and let me heal you.
I hate it because it caused me to look like the world, talk like the world, and get loose like the world.
I hate it because it controlled me by telling me I needed it to enjoy life. When rather it was separating me from truly tasting the beauty of life.
When you are a slave to something—that is not living.
I hate it because it wavered my decisions that always ended in more pain than I was experiencing in the first place. All will power would leave me. And I would react on any emotion that needed tending to when alone. We are called to *"take captive every thought to make it obedient to Christ." (2 Cor. 10:5)* It is almost impossible to rein in every thought while intoxicated and making them obedient to Christ. John Piper explains it this way: *Now I think that is the same obedience as in 2 Corinthians 10:4–5 when he brings our thoughts into*

obedience to Christ. And here he says, "I won't speak of anything except what Christ has accomplished." So that is what I am getting at when I say, expose yourself. Lay yourself open to the risen Christ by the power of the Holy Spirit through the words of the apostle Paul so that everything can be dismantled and then your brain, your mind, your thoughts can be taken captive and everything brought into conformity to Christ.

I hate it because it has involved all my worst decisions ever made.

When I got home from the store there was pain still haunting me. So I came out back, sat down, took a deep breath and the whistles and chirps of the birds began to calm me. And now the lightning bugs are flickering all around me. And the song by Britt Nicole, The Sun is Rising keeps playing in my head... *"You're gonna make it. You're gonna make it. The night can only last for so long."*

What do we really gain from being stubborn/prideful? I've learned all I gain is ending up right back where I left off in my sin the last time. My stubborn will has caused me to choose myself over others. My stubborn will has caused confusion, and confusion is not of the Lord. (1 Corinthians 14:33) My stubborn choices are not out of love, as love is not self-seeking. (1 Corinthians 13:5)
When you bury one stronghold, be alert and on guard for the next one to raise its nasty head.

A new normal will have to replace old habits.

It WILL pass. It is only a thought or urge. You are in control of your decision and actions. Let it pass. Let God fight for you. Do not let it defeat you anymore! Your decisions not only affect you but anyone close to you.

SEX: The Forbidden Taboo

"Shake yourself from the dust, rise up, O captive Jerusalem; Loose yourself from the chains around your neck, O captive daughter of Zion." (Isaiah 52:2 NASB)

Oh sex. Something given to be as a beautiful gift but rather it is abused and confused by most of the world. My X and I waited to have sex until our wedding night and it truly was beautiful; the way God intended it to be. But for some reason after my divorce my soul lost touch with my convictions of purity, self-worth, and Gods will. Sad to say once one mistake took place it was much easier to give into another one when home alone. This fake fulfillment became a slow drug that was killing me from the inside out.

However God never stopped pursuing. He never stopped loving me. He never stopped picking me back up when I was sobbing the next day all alone by my choices the night before. I can rejoice and say chains were literally broken and dropped to the dust at my feet. My heart and my flesh have closed the door to feeding my arousing feelings within for sex. It was nothing I did. It was the pure grace of God pursuing me. It was God never giving up on me. It was the constant pursuit of Him that got my attention. Is the fight over? No. But there is always good news with Christ.... *"The God of peace will soon crush Satan under your feet. The grace of our Lord Jesus Christ be with you" (Romans 16:20 ESV)* Call it what you want, but I am addicted to the presence of the Holy Spirit. He freed me and I will share it with all.

But as one door closes, and the enemy knows his deception is no longer going to work one way, he goes after another weakness that will keep us from getting to God. I love how Oswald Chambers puts it.... *"you have to wrestle against the things that prevent you from getting to God. We have not to put up a fight before God, not to wrestle with God, but to wrestle before God with things"* And any good wrestling match ends with defeat or victory. Which will it be for you? There are many victories even when there is a loss. Your loss could be your biggest gain.

Where are you with God today? Do you believe He is pursuing you right now? Do you believe He wants your whole heart, as He was the One that gave you your first heartbeat. His heart races for us. He longs for us to return to Him. Do you believe you are enough? You are enough sweet sister. He has never abandoned us. And He never will.

Stronghold of people pleasing and lack of identity turns into a trap of sexual temptation. Don't beat yourself up QUITE yet. ;) You are a warrior and warriors know who they are, what they need to defeat any battle, and who is not worth their time.

Identify and Admit those Dragons

"As a man thinks in his heart, so does he become." (Proverbs 23:7)

You will get what you go after, but the end result will not be what you truly want if searching to please the gratifications of your flesh. You are a sinner saved by grace. You are going to make unwise decisions on this new road of tasting singlehood all over again. But these decisions do not and will not define you if you choose to plant yourself in the truths of Scripture. His Word is waiting for us to embrace it, just as the way Jesus has embraced us. I completely understand all the admiration you are craving right now; especially if you have decided to not date quite yet. You want to be told you are beautiful. You want to have someone wrap their arm around you or gently rub your back. These are not bad things to want.

However, these thoughts we have to be cautious with though; as thoughts can turn into an obsession, and then that obsession takes action to achieve the restless soul within. Here is where we have to make a conscious decision; especially if you have already been here before. Whose attention are you seeking; and will it attract what you truly long for? Joyce Myers has written a whole book on the battlefield of the mind- but this one line about sums it all up for me... *"our actions are a direct result of our thoughts."*

Our thoughts may seem innocent for awhile; but where will you let them lead you. Will you let your thoughts stir up inside you actions that you would later regret?

What's it going to be ladies? Did you fall into temptation that is ripping you up inside, and think there is no way to keep moving forward? Are you going to set up boundaries, or just keep going back for more? We need to get more real with ourselves, and more real with others. The more we hide in our sin, the more we will not want to get out of bed, the more we will keep pursuing darkness, the more we will drift from God and the church. We are not promised butterflies and rainbows, we may even face rejection; this rejection is nothing new to Jesus. Will we live a life of being rejected or being the one that rejects the unconditional love and affection of our King? I much rather not put myself in a situation to be rejected by one that does not see the beauty inside me that is Jesus.

Many days are ahead where you continually will keep feeling rejected, but I am certain one day you will be accepted, pursued, and adored. The aroma of Christ is so sweet, mysterious, and only a true believer cannot resist more of that. Today all that matters is if you love well, forgive, and stay honest to the path you've been given to walk down. **You set yourself up for rejection when you run to the arms of ones that reject your deepest convictions within.** Run to the One that accepts your brokenness to turn it into a beautiful masterpiece.

Lets give that old life of iniquity, selfish deeds, sexual wanderings a good ole burial—move forward and onward to a life of Spirit filled decisions. Let us rejoice and dance and tell all how the good lord has renewed our soul. Time is passing quickly and our time is now—time to soar like an eagle above the storms, and when the vultures come in behind us chasing us to eat us up—fly toward the Son and put on your full armor of God as they will not be able to stand the blasts of heat that come from above.

Now that you have identified your strongholds it is time to be reminded of who you are. Just a heads up--You are a daughter of the King!

Identity

I see that the first trait to go to the gutter after divorce is our **identity**. There is so much confidence to be regained once we realize the constant, steadfast, and never changing relationship in the Holy Spirit. Too often He is rejected; where all He wants is for us to engage into the most satisfying relationship with Him.

Do you want to go deeper with The Spirit? Let us begin praying this simple prayer together each morning. Write it down and put it by your bed somewhere, before your feet hit the ground you utter these words to the One that fashioned us with delicate care.

Lord sweet Jesus take me deeper into the knowledge of who you are. Complete me by taking away any strongholds that are hindering the most fulfilling relationship I could be enjoying with You. Lord—I surrender my life to you. I am yours. Take me and do with me what you will. Dwell in my home; make this a place of refuge. Be my shield and strength this day. Be my confidence. Be my joy. Be the One that I run to first. In the name of Jesus—Amen.

Confidence in your Identity fights off the strongholds that want to steal, kill, and destroy you. Demolish the lies regain your pride. Restoration has been part of your voyage all along.

Dear sweet one that feels their life sucks right now, the sun will shine again, and not only will you see it shining, you will feel it again. You will soak it up, breathe it in, and smile while exhaling. I look at this time of singleness as a way of God reminding me how much He enjoys me walking with Him. At one time that is all Adam did in the Garden of Eden; he walked with the Alpha and Omega. And then God saw it was not good for man to be alone; and we know the rest of the story. Ever since the day brokenness and shame entered the world our souls have not been at rest. Because they are being called back to the One that created us to walk hand in hand with Him every step of the way. Why do you think we like to be heard when we speak, because our Creator made us to be attentive to Him, to desire companionship, to live life alongside the One that died for us so we could live for Him. Once we get to a place of contentment with our life circumstances, we are able to live without fear of the unknown. While living in fear only keeps us further from truly living. We miss out on the ultimate life lesson—living by faith and not sight.

Don't lie to one another. You're done with that old life. It's like a filthy set of ill-fitting clothes you've stripped off and put in the fire. Now you're dressed in a new wardrobe. Every item of your new way of life is custom-made by the Creator, with his label on it. All the old fashions are now obsolete.
(Colossians 3:9-10) The Message

Honest Wanderer

One of the healthiest choices you can make is becoming honest with yourself. There were days I would hit rock bottom and say to myself; I am not lost, but my soul wants to wander away from the truths of knowing I am found. I mentioned to a dear friend that I feel lost when I am not being a momma. And her response was, **"but maybe that's the lesson, find yourself"** And to most people that sounds empowering and a lesson most want to pursue and find; but I find myself thinking quite the opposite. So far I have learned the lesson has nothing to do with me, but all the more with seeking with all my heart, mind, and body who our Creator is. I am and will always be a mother, just as God will always be our Father. Even when we are distant from Him, He still remains the same in His care and concern for our well-being. When I am not in my children's physical reach I still can be conditioning my motherhood through my worship with the Lord. **The more I massage the heart He came into, the overflow of His love will give me that much more strength to be the woman and mother God created me to be for my children.**

He is not surprised by any of our circumstances; He simply is just waiting for us to let Him be the center of our lives. He is waiting for us to find Him, follow Him, and to never look back at the old ways of life indulging in self-gratification. Jesus said...come with me, follow me, lose yourself... *"If anyone serves me, he must follow me; and where I am, there will my servant be also. If anyone serves me, the Father will honor him." (John 12:26) ESV*

We are not asked to serve ourselves, we are called to be His servant that follows His lead. And when we are serving the One that created us and knit us together in our mothers womb, slowly the deception of believing we need to find who we are will turn more into who am I in Christ. We will not be able to find ourselves without knowing who God is first, and who we are in Christ. Because we are created in Him image.

"The thief comes only to steal and kill and destroy. I came that they may have life and have it abundantly." (John 10:10)

The thief wants to continue in his pursuit to steal as much as possible from you, and the first place he throws a dart to is our identity. The deceiver wants us to forget who we are in Christ. And will come at every angle to get us to believe finding who we are as an individual without Christ.

Marriage takes a lot from our individuality and we are capable of losing touch with who we once were before becoming one with another. And today we must not look back to who we use to be, because that person no longer exists. Whether you may like admitting it or not-your x spouse brought out a better you. I do not know your story, and I understand many get into a relationship that is abusive; but today you have to believe you are not your past and you did not make that person abuse you or leave you. We are responsible for us. And you taking the stand to remove yourself from an unhealthy home should remind you that—"*you are an overcomer by the blood of the Lamb and a conqueror through Him Who loves me.*" (Romans 8:37, Revelation 12:11)

It may take many months or years to see how they opened new doors for you to see the light in a different way. But any wound that has taken place will be healed. The question you have to ask yourself today is, who will we allow to heal our wounds? God has brought us to this wilderness to heal us. I know that if I am having open heart surgery I want the best surgeon in the country. God wants to be our professional surgeon in this time of healing. **A lot will be said of our character in how we deal with the change of who we are today without a significant other**. This time in our wilderness is a chance to seek how we see ourselves in Christ.

Timothy Keller makes me think a little deeper on this quote from his book, The Meaning of Marriage....

"It seems almost oxymoronic to believe that this new idealism has led to a new pessimism about marriage, but that is exactly what has happened. In generations past there was far less talk about "compatibility" and finding the ideal soul mate. Today we are looking for someone who accepts us as we are and fulfills our desires, and this creates an unrealistic set of expectations that frustrates both the searchers and the searched for."

But if we really think about this way of viewing compatibility; deep down if we want someone to love us for who we are, and accept us for our flaws and any other hindrance to our conscious—don't we need to first identify our flaws and know who we are as an individual before entering into a relationship of unrealistic expectations. Sounds like a time bomb waiting to explode to me. We as individuals get too caught up in our mistakes, flaws, competition with others, success, and our appearance as being our identity. This becomes a waste of time when that is the sole focus of your purpose in life. Rather—we as Christians should be focusing on all the powerful traits we share with Christ. Since I cannot sit here and speak to you directly by name I want you to find your identity below and begin healing by the truth of who you are in Christ. God does not want you to live in fear, pain, deception, lies, and defeat any longer. When you come to the identity that you know is yours—write it down big and put it up on your bathroom mirror, in your car, and on the refrigerator.

To the one that committed adultery and repented but was not forgiven...
- *"I have put off the old man and have put on the new man, which is renewed in the knowledge after the image of Him Who created me." (Colossians 3:9-10)*
- *"I am holy and without blame before Him in love" (Ephesians 1:4; 1 Peter 1:16)*

To the one that was left for another lover...
- *"I am complete in Him Who is the Head of all principality and power" (Colossians 2:10)*
- *"I can do all things through Christ Jesus" (Philippians 4:13)*
- *"I am part of a chosen generation, a royal priesthood, a holy nation, a purchased people" (1 Peter 2:9)*

To the one that was abused mentally and/or physically...

- "I am far from oppression, and fear does not come near me." (Isaiah 54:14)
- "I can quench all the fiery darts of the wicked one with my shield of faith" (Ephesians 6:16)
- "I am born of God, and the evil one does not touch me." (1 John 5:18)

To the one that still can't figure out why their marriage ended...
- "I have the peace of God that passes all understanding." (Philippians 4:7)
- "I have the mind of Christ." (1 Corinthians 2:16; Philippians 4:7)
- "I am a believer, and the light of the Gospel shines in my mind." (2 Corinthians 4:4)

Do not love the world or anything in the world. If anyone loves the world, love for the Father is not in them (1 John 2:15)

The pain that stings deep within my heart makes me stop and evaluate. "Search me, O God, and know my heart! Try me and know my thoughts." (Psalm 139;23)
I want to be poured out like a drink offering. And John Piper has given me much ammunition on how to pursue this desire deep down in my soul. He says, *"we need to ponder the superiority of God as our great reward over all that the world has to offer"* Piper also challenged me to ask myself; what tangible objects or conversations do I have present in my life that are hindering my complete devotion to God. And each time I think a release of sexual tension with another man, a drink of wine to get me lose from my pains, and a simple conversation to exchange good feelings with the opposite sex I need to remind myself, death will take each and every one of them. None of those are acts of worship, but rather <u>steps toward being choked</u> from truly living in freedom.
And Romans 8:13 proves this point... *"For if you live according to the flesh you will die, but if by the Spirit you put to death the deeds of the body, you will live."* It is up to us to take a step toward eternal joy, and it all weighs on todays choice of living for the flesh or The Spirit.

What does your faith reveal about your desires?

Do you desire to be comforted by what the world has to offer?

Or are you seeking with all your heart, soul, and mind to understand the depths and beauty of our Creator and Savior?

Branded: By the Big (D)ADDY in Heaven

So here we are living in this world, but called to be set apart from it. And now feeling branded by the world as being divorced. But really quick, I am going to adjust the so called scarlett letter of D for Divorce to the Big D for our DADDY in heaven!! You're a daughter of the King and He has branded you as his DAUGHTER. Even though we may look as the world, we get to choose if want to move forward looking like the world in our choice of living. We get to choose if we let the world tell us we are a failure because we did not keep our marriage alive. **We are defined by our identity in Christ**—never ever by the things of this world. And we will find this to be true when we give over our pride and let God be our leader, provider, lover, sustainer, protector, and healer. Slowly but surely the Lord has been stripping me from certain loves of this world, and the further I get away from desiring the world, the closer I get to feeling His presence and only wanting Him as the love of my life. I am tired of hearing people say, "God will provide the perfect man for you in His timing." This desire has become very low on my lists of wants, as I realize the focus of me wanting a man over God is loving the world, and if I love the world more than God, the love of the Father is not in me. And if I do not have the love of the Father in me I cannot adequately love another man. I much rather focus all my energy into loving the Father I am going to be worshipping for eternity.
If God sees fit to bring another man to be my earthly protector and provider then that is His business. Just as when God saw it was not good for Adam to be alone, He provided him a mate. Adam did not ask of this, God gave this to him willfully as a gift. The only gift my soul finds peace with is being fully committed to the service of Jesus. And I will rest in this peace as Gods calling on my life in this wilderness of sanctification. Faithful acts of obedience slowly soften the bitter hearted. All you can do is move forward toward a life that pleases the Lord. Even when there is nothing given back in return, remember where your identity resides.

Confidence: Your Greatest Weapon

"You were running well. Who hindered you from obeying the truth? This persuasion is not from him who calls you. A little leaven leavens the whole lump" (Galatians 5:7-9 ESV)

There will be detours in our life that may slow our pilgrimage down, but they are never a dead end. Rather looking at this day as a dead end lets prepare our hearts for a wow moment. **What may seem like a delay in our journey is really Gods way of showing us how cautious He is with the mending of our hearts.**

When one runs to the arms of a gentleman of the night one does not walk confidently in who they are. It reveals where you put your worth as an individual.

You have lost hope.

You have no peace.

You are scared to face your pain.

You must change your mindset and say with confidence:

I not only hope but I believe there is light despite all the darkness. Once you believe in the hope to come the peace you breathe in will become your confidence. And when you walk in confidence you will set your eyes and be focused on who you are in Christ. That purpose is your identity and that identity will be your joy.

*This **mystery**, which is Christ in you, the **hope** of glory.*
Colossians 1:27

Confusion clearly fogs you from the hope God wants to gift you with. The chief of lies wants to warp your mind into believing you have no purpose anymore. These are clear signs the enemy is confusing you with traps.

Distracted, embarrassed, turmoil in your gut, agitation, blurring of convictions, clouded vision, unsettling thoughts, anxious. Your confidence has been shaken but not destroyed.

"If only the LORD had killed us back in Egypt," they moaned. "There we sat around pots filled with meat and ate all the bread we wanted. But now you have brought us into this wilderness to starve us all to death." (Exodus 16:3)

The Israelites passed down some familiar traits we all know a little too well. We can all relate with wanting to go back to our old ways as they brought a sense of belonging, an odd feeling of security, and our cravings fulfilled. And when God takes us from our bondage, it takes faith to start all over and to begin living a new life of moving forward. A life that requires taking daily steps of faith. We cannot expect a new year to change how we respond to the desires of our flesh. We have to make a choice to not look back on what was once our bondage. **When we look back, it is opening a door to let it back in**. The more you think on someone or something that will not bring glory to God cast it out and know those chains have been broken, and they can not have you any longer.
I know how to open a door way too easily when prone to wander. I know what I want, and will do what it takes to get it. The day after I was in deep sorrow I met up with someone that came across to me as a great guy, but come to find out he is lower than scum and took advantage of a vulnerable woman who didn't want to be alone that night. The next night after not

hearing from him I drank myself a whole bottle of wine and put myself to bed. Treasures of this world will only weigh our soul down, empty my soul sweet Jesus.

This morning when I woke up I had already missed the first service of church, and the second service started in 30 minutes. God told me to get my butt to church, well not those exact words, but the spirit was thick upon me and I made it to service right when the music was beginning. And I am not 100% I even brushed my teeth, and I was singing at the top of my lungs, maybe that's why the lady next to me moved seats. No joke.

But in all seriousness, **when the spirit prompts you to move, sprint to Him and expect the unimaginable to happen.** And let me tell you, todays message had my name written all over it. It all began with **Exodus 14:3, "they are wandering in the land; the wilderness has shut them in."** God takes us from bondage and leads us to a land of milk and honey, but this wilderness we have been lead to takes trusting the Lord. Trust is the greatest gift we can give back to God. He has already given us the greatest gift, His Son. How come we cannot be selfless as His Son and give him the gift of trust. He is not asking us to trust Him to harm us, but to give us a land of pure satisfaction that is way sweeter than anything we put our lips to, we stroke with our hands, and watch with our eyes.

Every time we run back to our old ways, we are doubting the good God is leading us to. **He wants to settle the doubt, so our faith can grow**. God has lead me to this wilderness of singlehood to shape my faith. Is this ringing true to your soul as well? **The wilderness is not a place for God to harm us, but a place to reveal His love and power to us. Don't think of it as aimlessly wandering but faithfully voyaging.** The more I give into my fear of being alone, the more apt I am to submit to the fear, rather than the will of God.

The wilderness is meant to be a....
- Beautiful place of refining
- Growing season in our faith
- Watching God move mountains

- Seeing Him light up the sky when we feel darkness all around us.
- Letting Him provide for our needs not our wants and desires
- Reminding us of His steadfast love

I pray you do not lose sight of your wildernesses calling. When we wake up and realize the wilderness God has brought us to is a gift rather than a curse we will truly begin to live freely. One day we will look back on this season and miss it. Lets hold on tight to Gods hand and never look back, but only looking forward.

What wilderness has the Lord lead you to but have been too blind by your sin/pain to notice the manna right in front of you? He has given you all you need this day; nothing more nothing less.

This pilgrimage we are embracing may feel like a prison at times. Merely we are the only ones closing the door and locking ourselves in from the beauty God wants to lead us to. As there are days when the reality of it all strikes my heart and wants to close me in and feed off the heaviness. I remind **myself we are in control of the walls we build for ourselves.** The more honest I am with myself, the easier it is to be honest with others. If it were not for my decisions I made in the past, I would not be experiencing this wilderness of refining. This is my wilderness and I want to guard it by not letting in what God does not want, and not taking too much of a blessing that could spoil if abused.

This is only part of our journey—it will not last forever.

I no longer live in fear of my past, as that became a wall and blocked the beauty of Gods grace on my life. Living in fear of what others think of us steals Gods glory. The last thing God wants is for us to live in fear when the first thing He wants to do is be our confidence. And **confidence always outweighs fear**. But be careful with the difference of being confident and arrogant. Confidence we put our trust in God. Arrogance we put our trust in ourselves.

"Open up before God, keep nothing back; he"ll do whatever needs to be done: He'll validate your life in the clear light of day and stamp you with approval at high noon." (Psalm 37:4-5 The MSG)

Embrace the good days when all is well with your soul. Notice what has changed or what you became freed from. Good days do not come by chance they are given when we keep our minds on His love. We trust Him so we walk confidently toward a life of freedom. Do not pick back up what you have already laid down at His feet.

    Yesterday I had a deep burning desire to run in a big open field of wildflowers with my arms raised high, twirling in a sundress with the sun shining down on me. Why? I really don't know, but I sense it as a calling from God to run to me, embrace me, dance with me, smile with me.....draw near to me....come to me.....dance like nobody is watching, let it all go, and give it to Me. It is a freeing feeling. and it is only noon as I write this, the day is young and I may just go do this...
    We are all on a journey being lead to freedom, but why not run to our Father today so desperately with delight. Delight: this is the word of the day. This word has been released to the Lord in prayer today as I am seeking Him to be my go to delight and desire.
"Delight yourself in the Lord, and he will give you the desires of your heart. Commit your way to the Lord; trust in him, and he will act." (Psalm 37:4-5)
When you think of delighting in something, how would you describe how that would look or feel? When I am delighting in snuggling with my children, I soak it in by breathing in the smell of their hair, the touch of their sticky fingers or soft skin of their cheek, I let their giggles or breathing sound out every

other noise around, and when I kiss them tenderly I taste the sweetness, maybe leftover peanut-butter, or snot. but all sweet to me because they are part of me, and I study the shape of their profile and hold on as tight as they let me before they say, "mommy you are crushing me" ;) When we truly delight in something or someone we engage every sense we are capable using. We touch it, we smell it, we look at it, we taste it, and we listen.

We dive in, we give it our all to get out of it the most we can to give us some sort of life, some sort of satisfaction, and joy. I mean I can not help to think about when I eat a warm piece of peach cobbler with ice cream on top, melting, then it perfectly dissolves in my mouth. I savor it when I put it in my mouth...I want it to last.

I am overwhelmed by the presence of God today. I asked and He showed up. I can not get enough of Him. I can not type fast enough as my heart races of contentment for Him, and Him alone. I can not get close enough to Him. I want more. And He is active and pouring His love out on me. He is enough. He is love. I was made for love. I am a lover of your presence. (I am singing right now in between lines, lifting my hands to Him rejoicing on how I am a lover of His presence.....oh my goodness...He is here......just to see your face)

Waiting will come easier once you can admit your strongholds, know who you are in Christ, and realize you are not alone.

WAIT: Don't Settle
Yea...this is when you probably wont like me so much.

What is a year to God, really?!
I know for me it felt like a lifetime.

I can't sit here and tell you what to do with your love life but I can hopefully plant a seed for holding off to the lure of adoration from man.

It may take you getting to the grass you thought was so much sweeter on the other side just to realize you have much healing and rebuilding to do in yourself. I just want to save women from added heartache and learn from my ignorant mistakes. The last thing I want for you is to feel like a failure all over again, not feel wanted all over again, and new walls be formed because you ran to the arms of the night, rather to the arms of THE LIGHT.
You know what it takes to be committed and it'll come natural to make yourself at home as this is all you have known the past so many years you were married. But lets be honest, if you have gotten yourself out there already, which I am guessing you have if you are reading this book; dating in your 30's is way different than dating in your 20's. In your 30's life is more established and settled, but that does not mean you have to SETTLE for anything less than you know you deserve.

 I am moved by Elisabeth Elliot's wisdom—*"struggling is simply delayed obedience."* It has taken me a long time to get here and say this; we never will get that peace we desire until we give ourselves over to the calling God has on our life. It doesn't mean our hearts won't ache for that fleshly desire, but we can know for sure God has something way sweeter for us than we can imagine.

The Lord had already blessed me with one husband, and now two children. How selfish of me to want more, and to want it so quickly again. And who is to say this is what God has for me again. I think it is easy for people to not know what to say, and to fill the void of loneliness—the "obvious" answer would be, "God has another man out there for you, one that will share your same values, one that will love you..." I can honestly say for the first time, if this is what God has for me great, if not...I am content with that as well. I am no longer looking, no longer wondering, no longer flirting with the idea of another man coming into my life. I was made for love. I was made for loving God.

I wish it was a quick healing process but it has taken me almost three years to get where I am today.

Everyone's healing process is going to be different. I was in denial for almost 7 months. I caught myself thinking
"He will come back"
"There is no way this can happen to me"
"I cant' be a divorced woman"
"We made a commitment to God"
"He will come back......he has to...."

And slowly once I realized my marriage was going to end in divorce the alcohol became a good friend, church became non-existent, and I started putting myself out there. It was a quick death as God was never giving me peace with any of these decisions. Red flags everywhere, stomach in knots, and me just doing whatever felt good at the moment, which then got me to July 27, 2014. But, as you saw I STILL was not ready for commitment and giving up my fleshly desires, but once again God waited on me to return, to pick me back up and was ready when I was ready to give him my WHOLE heart.

"If you love me, you will obey what I command" John 14:15

As often as I think it be nice to love someone again, God whispers... Love me. And by me obeying His commands, I am loving Him. And by obeying His commands I am reminded that He has something way better for me in His time. I must rest in that and trust that. Too often people rush into a relationship as I understand why, but why not wait and heal first so one day we can give our heart fully to God and another man if blessed with that. Not just little pieces that are leftover. Would you like someone giving you their leftovers?

And I also look at this lesson as learning to obey God and follow His leading as preparation to follow the lead of a future husband. I will admit, I do not like being told no, and I am quite stubborn. When it is not going my way, I either just do what I want anyways, or make a fit until I get what I want. (not real attractive, right?) And I am learning really fast, that does not go over well with God. He will just keep on being persistent until He breaks us of our will of disobedience. I am slowly learning to be content with what I have in front of me this day, not panicking and reaching for what I don't have.

Let me lead you to an analogy the Lord placed on my heart that helped me realize my lack of waiting.

Ever been locked out of your house? Or even worse been locked out with only your car key in hand? Try putting that key in the lock to get in your home... As hard as you try to get it to fit, it's just not going to budge, nor fit. Because that key was not made for this door. Are you following me? How often do we keep going back to that same door with the wrong key, not able to get to the other side because you are trying to make it happen with the wrong tool. Panic slowly rises... And frustration.... Then maybe you're so determined to make it happen you take the screen off your window and climb into a window that was "left open." You made it in. But did you get the satisfaction you were looking for? It took a lot of effort and damage to your home. If only we waited for God to bring along the perfect key to open the door to contentment and joy.

Will you wait on the Lord?

What are you willing to hold off on today?

If I can save just one woman from the traps of giving her body away emotionally or physically then I know that me sharing my failures with you was not a waste. As I desire for Him to have complete glory as He saved me, and I rejoice with the words of David in Psalm 30:

I will exalt you, Lord,
for you lifted me out of the depths
and did not let my enemies gloat over me.
Lord my God, I called to you for help,
and you healed me.
You, Lord, brought me up from the realm of the dead;
you spared me from going down to the pit.
Sing the praises of the Lord, you his faithful people;
praise his holy name.
For his anger lasts only a moment,
but his favor lasts a lifetime;
weeping may stay for the night,
but rejoicing comes in the morning.
When I felt secure, I said,

> *"I will never be shaken."*
> *Lord, when you favored me,*
> *you made my royal mountain stand firm;*
> *but when you hid your face,*
> *I was dismayed.*
> *To you, Lord, I called;*
> *to the Lord I cried for mercy:*
> *"What is gained if I am silenced,*
> *if I go down to the pit?*
> *Will the dust praise you?*
> *Will it proclaim your faithfulness?*
> *Hear, Lord, and be merciful to me;*
> *Lord, be my help."*
> *You turned my wailing into dancing;*
> *you removed my sackcloth and clothed me with joy,*
> *that my heart may sing your praises and not be silent.*
> *Lord my God, I will praise you forever.*

Once you believe how important, loveable, precious, and chosen you are the dwelling of the Holy Spirit will feel more secure and radiate through you. When I envision my heart being guarded, the imagery that comes to mind is a stationed angel-cherubim and a revolving sword of fire, protecting the path to my heart of life. That's how serious God was when he kicked out Adam and Eve with the tree of life; as we should be with our vulnerable hearts.

> *"Indeed, we felt that we had received the sentence of death. But that was to make us rely not on ourselves but on God who raises the dead." (2 Corinthians 1:9)*

I never want to lose this desperation I have for the Lord. The tears Jesus shed for you and me tasted just as bittersweet to Him as our tears taste to us. I cannot help to feel more one with the Lord sharing tears in the same way. Tears are a sign of letting ourselves release the pain that shreds our heart to pieces. If I can encourage you this day; let God heal your pain. How you ask? You have to be still. You have to wait. And as hard as this will be, you will have to give up seeking affection from men. It will not heal you. Guess what—I know what you are thinking. Let me guess....

"I deserve this"

"I am ready to see if I still got what it takes"

"I want to feel admired and beautiful"

"It's been years since I have had sex, and I am ready to feel sexy again"

Or you're stubborn like I have been the past year, and really like all the things I am saying, but will take pieces here and there and apply to you what feels good. But, you still plan on living the way you want to, because you do not want to take the time to slow down and really get to the issue of your pain. **We have to face our pain to be able to move forward in any other type of relationship.** If not, we end up adding more infection to the wound that is already gaping open. Can you please trust me on this one? I wish I could hold your hand and walk you step by step in this journey. But, God already has that taken care of. And I hope you can feel my sincere request to seek out what God is trying to mend up for you.

I know you want a companion. I know you are lonely. I know your bed is cold at night. I know you're really not that hungry, but have looked in the pantry and refrigerator a dozen times and still nothing looks appetizing. I know you have become a professional bug killer. I know you feel like your friendships have changed; but what better time than now to find out who

your true friends are. I feel your pain, even as I write my heart is aching.
I know you will do what you want. I know you will have many times of weakness, as we have so many easy band-aids we can run to whenever we want.

Today I ask—what is God asking of you to do with your pain?

"No good thing does he withhold from those who walk uprightly." (Ps. 84:11 ESV)

Reread the scripture. Not one good thing does he withhold from ones that walk uprightly... now look up and around you. What good things are right in front of you that you can thank God for? Now write them down. Or maybe you are having a really hard day today and can barely get yourself out of bed. Is your bible close by? Can you reach for it right now, open it up to Psalm 84:11 and let the Word comfort you, breathe it in, soak it up and write down how you are thankful for Gods Word. May His word be your good thing today, and let the rest of your day feed off this truth.

Anytime my mind or inner desires of wanting to be comforted by a man lately I have been slowly redirecting my mind to quoting this scripture—*"no good thing does he withhold from me"* This inner war I mentioned earlier will rage against our soul everyday, and lust will deceive us into feeling we are missing out on a greater satisfaction if we let it. And can I just say, me even writing this is huge as I believed that lie for so long. If it raged within, I followed its desire because I knew it would feel good. Rather I should have been letting Gods word feed my appetite for Him, as <u>its power would wean my heart from the ambiguous taste of lust.</u>

"As a dog returns to its vomit, so fools repeat their folly."
(Proverbs 26:11)

Yesterday I shot a series of photos that shared a glimpse of this journey I have been sharing. If you are interested in seeing all the images go to my blog; www.annapociaskphotography.com and the title is, *I've been such a mess.* I am curious as to what you see when you look at this image above.

What I see is desperation. Someone running back for more answers, answers that will not satisfy, but only leave her all alone. And possibly drive her crazy.

This was me so many times. I would scrummage and dig to find answers in all the wrong places, and I was slowly killing myself within. At the time I was clueless to the bondage that was weighing me down, keeping me from church and friends months ago. I am pretty sure I hibernated for 8 months.

However the beauty in all of this mess was everytime I ran to the worldly pleasures, God never stopped running after my heart. His pursuit for me makes my heart sing, makes me want to scream it from the rooftops to everyone I meet. I want people to say to themselves, there is something different about that girl. And that difference be my reliance and love I have for God.

When I shot this series of photos I had been seeking how to be content in the Lord. And it hit me, **true attraction from another comes when we are most content with who we are.** Are you desiring a companion but running yourself to a ditch of despair? That right person will come when you are able to realize being content is beautiful. **Contentment attracts the right people.**

Can you write down things or people in your life right now that are causing discontentment?
Begin sifting them out and start seeing a new life of peace and contentment. And let God do the rest. When you finally can look at a guy without thinking he could be a possible mate you are on the right road to freedom, a road of contentment. Will you take a moment to sit still and wait on the Lords best for your life? He will bring your best to you. Run to Him.

There is no fear in love, but perfect love casts out fear. For fear has to do with punishment, and whoever fears has not been perfected in love. (1 John 4:18)

Ponder with me on Elizabeth Elliot's wisdom on love... *"To love means to open ourselves to suffering. Shall we shut our doors to love, then, and be "safe"?"*

It seems there are different plateaus in ones lifetime when ready to dive in head first, blindfolded, and into the depths of the never-ending sea for that search of love. We remember our first "love" or what I like to call an infatuation with our mysterious hormones. Then another climax when off to college, the years of pursuing the MRS degree and finding "the one". And a third is added to this blinded sort of love—post divorce.

As quickly we are ready to dive into this mysterious feeling of love we need to be just as ready to undergo trials that will stretch our faith.

It is almost impossible for females to grow up without being distracted by the fantasy of making a home of their own. Then when off to college the distraction continues as one believes their biological clock is ticking, and if the one isn't found in college you are doomed. Our world thrives off that spark of romance—and depending on how much one is desperate for it; they will go as far as seeking it out through a one night stand, lead one on just to get fed compliments, getting physical, and watching TV shows that rile up emotions that need not be. This type of spark will quickly die out, as a fire needs tender care to keep it going once activated. I would not know this if it was not for all the fires I have been making this week for the kids and I. I have learned when working with firewood; you can't just light it up once, walk away and expect to come back to the relaxing crackling noise it gives off, beautiful amber glowing, and just the right temperature burning. I have not perfected my campfire skills quite yet, but, each day I have learned a new way to get it burning just perfect for us to enjoy. I have to fan it to give the fire more oxygen to breathe, poke the coals once they begin breaking off, add more paper, and usually takes a few splashes of lighter fluid to get down into the wood. I love thinking of this scenario in ones search of a relationship. And as we all know when we let our guard down, and are not cautious we get burned. That is why it is important to study the fire that has begun, and seek out if the spark is genuine and in line with your convictions. Or is this a fire that is going to get out of control, burn everything around you and be only left with the ash of pain. We never know how a spark will end as it is our responsibility to guard it, tend to it, enjoy it, and put it out quickly when we know deep down there will not be any fruit.

How is the equilibrium found in our daily search of love? Our soul will find rest from the worldly searching when we realize all God asks of us is to abandon our lives to Him. This morning before I began writing, my words uttered to Him.... "Lord I sit at your throne thanking you for being my Provider, I surrender to You this day, have your way with me." The kilter will feel off for awhile if coming out of a marriage as the adjustment of new schedules are placed with children, an even number turned to an individual, but I can not sit here typing anymore as my heart bursts with joy of saying—God is steadfast, constant, always with us, He is the only One that can make us complete. He never intended for a spouse to fill our every need.

God created us to be our Protector, to provide for us, to draw us to Him, so we can experience His love. We find in Exodus 34:14.... *"You must worship no other gods, for the LORD, whose very name is Jealous, is a God who is jealous about his relationship with you."* This is not a jealousy we are familiar with, this is a jealousy of guarding what is dear to Him. If you are here, you more than likely have been wounded by a relationship that at one time was your everything. I can assure you, you are in the safe arms of Jesus.

"Beloved, I urge you as sojourners and exiles to abstain from the passions of the flesh, which wage war against your soul"
(1 Peter 2:11)

I believe if I were not taking an anti-depressant I would be weeping right now as this verse came alive to me for the first time. I began searching for a devotion with the topic being, *passion* from John Pipers; Solid Joys. Before the search I was seeking to find a scripture that pertained to the zeal I desired for the Lord; but always seem to get more wrapped up in the intense emotion of man. The enticement of man 9 out of 10 times always wins. And I am plain tired of it. How about you? I wanted the Lord to give me a word that gave me way to a thought that has been stirring within me the past week.

How would our lives look spiritually if we dedicated as much thought, passion, and time into making ourselves available to God rather than the nearest single giving us attention?

We never know how God is going to get our attention, but I know too well it typically is when we are ready to put forth the effort of going to war with the distractions that wage havoc against our soul. We all know what happens in war; and this war for companionship that wants your soul is not willing to go down without a fight. And it doesn't help when everyone around you keeps trying to hook you up with a friend, telling you there is someone out there perfect for you, or there are many fish in the sea.... When desperately your soul is crying out for you to slow down; hence the lack of real joy you may experiencing. If you are anxious once you get to a healthy content place you must still keep seeking out these emotions. Anything we ignore during our pilgrimage that needs dealt with will only be carried into another relationship. You and I both know we don't want that.
Lets get to the meat of our dead souls. The truth of the matter is that a part of your soul **feels** dead and desperately wants revived. This is what brings me to shear fear and trembling, oh yeah and disgust. When we give into the lusts of man, by

giving our body over to another, this is why our soul literally dies. It becomes cut off from the Spirit, because it cannot be in communion with sin.

Those who sow in tears
shall reap with shouts of joy!
He who goes out weeping,
bearing the seed for sowing,
shall come home with shouts of joy,
bringing his sheaves with him. Psalm 126:5-6 (ESV)

When the morning light began to slowly grace my room and the birds were chirping I laid there on my back asking the Spirit to be my everything today, to come alive in me as it did the day I mentioned while sitting at the table.
And the Lord graciously entered my soul, as I felt the peace in my heart. The Lord is my rock as I have never felt more focused on the priorities in my life.
And I seriously felt my heart wanting to go on lock down and handing over the key to the One who created my heart. I wholeheartedly trust when He wants to unlock it I will rise, walk with Him hand in hand, until He takes my hand and places it in the hands of the man He desires for me to be a helpmate for. And for the man he chooses to protect me and to never give up on me. When this heart wants to be pursued, they will have to go through God first.
My soul has been quieted, as my heart is being tenderized, seasoned, and waiting to be enjoyed with pure delight. I will wait Lord. I am yours. Swoon me Lord with your delicate presence that my heart ever so desires. Keep me still Lord, keep me steady and focused, and keep me calm and not aroused to the arousal of my flesh.
Yes Lord as I sit here I envision restoration in ripped apart souls. I see victory to come for the ones that are left standing at the altar with their spouse no longer being their shield and protector, encourager and supporter.
Weary one, I trust that if you are here so far into these pages of my journey, you are "fighting the good fight of faith; laying hold of eternal life." (1 Timothy 6:12) You desire so much more than what this world has to offer, and your soul cries out for you to take hold of The Spirit and let it jolt you into the most amazing ride of your life.

How much do you trust Him with the heart He fashioned and intricately designed for you?

Are you willing to let go of any ties that are keeping you from truly experiencing the love of the Lord? Will you trust?

"It's who you are and the way you live that count before God. Your worship must engage your spirit in the pursuit of truth. That's the kind of people the Father is out looking for: those who are simply and honestly themselves before him in their worship. God is sheer being itself—Spirit. Those who worship him must do it out of their very being, their spirits, their true selves, in adoration." (John 4:23-24 The MSG)

My prayer this day is simply put: may I desire to hear from the Lord more than wanting to hear from man. Dear sweet Spirit enlighten the eyes of my heart to know you deeper. Ask for the moon, ladies. These desires are not stirred without a purpose.

As the morning progressed my mind was being tempted by the lure of adoration from man. And I had to ask myself a hard question. Why do I want a man that lacks the most important attribute to my life? Why not trust if God can give me such a sweet friendship with a man now, why wouldn't He give me the whole package that included a passion to live for the Lord? The eyes of my heart were awoken a few weeks ago, and the decision to say goodbye to an old friend I had been connecting and being challenged with mentally and creatively. The intensions were pure and innocent; just carrying on daily conversation. But as time went on, every waking moment began to be fogged with wanting his pursuit, attention, and poetic words.
The Lord knew this journey would exhaust me and be difficult; but He called me to it because He believed in me enough that I would never give up. He knew when He called me to this journey I would grit my teeth and take it on as more of a duty, but toward the end seeing it turn into a delight to be on this trek.
The Lord has heard my cry and found delight in my request. As Timothy Keller puts it, *"prayer is simply a recognition of the greatness of God."* (pg 26 in the book Prayer) When I sought Him out this morning to be more infatuated with hearing from Him my evening has ended with a bubbling over of joy for His presence. He let me struggle for a bit, but then

the assurance of His presence was so much sweeter there was no hesitation to want man over God.

If you are on the fence about breaking an emotional attachment with another that is unequally yoked with your beliefs I will direct your heart to the living and active word of God:

> *Don't become partners with those who reject God. How can you make a partnership out of right and wrong? That's not partnership; that's war. Is light best friends with dark? Does Christ go strolling with the Devil? Do trust and mistrust hold hands? Who would think of setting up pagan idols in God's holy Temple? But that is exactly what we are, each of us a temple in whom God lives. God himself put it this way:*
>
> *"I'll live in them, move into them;*
> *I'll be their God and they'll be my people.*
> *So leave the corruption and compromise;*
> *leave it for good," says God.*
> *"Don't link up with those who will pollute you.*
> *I want you all for myself. (2 Corinthians 6:14-17 The MSG)*

I get it. You want him to come to know the Lord and have what you experience spiritually. It is not up to us, so please take that burden off of you and distraction that's keeping you from living in freedom. This will become a slow death if you stay here any longer, dead weight spiritually if you will. Another lie that I am sure you are aware of that is confirmation to end this separation anxiety you are dealing with. When you tell yourself, but we connect on so many levels and he really gets me, listens to me, challenges me, adores me, laughs uncontrollably with me. Why am I mentioning separation anxiety—don't only toddlers deal with this when they cannot fathom the thought of being apart from the one that nurtures them? **A good way to test if you are staying in an unyoked relationship is by the very thought of not having this person in your life leaves you feeling lost,**

broken, knots in your stomach, not able to eat, cannot live without him are all sheer signs this person has become more of a substitute than one that leads you to a life of stability, balance, teamwork, and oneness in Christ.

I will encourage you to write out a list of the most important traits you want in a spouse. You will need to disengage your desires for whomever you may be unyoked with when writing these out. Ask the Lord to direct your desires and write them down. Once you are done, how many add up that invite the unyoked individual into your life.

Sweet Jesus, grant me to desire what you desire. As much as I want to write out what I would want in a teammate, my heart is not at ease as of yet to focus on that now. Jesus is not done with me yet. As He is a jealous God and has been fighting passionately for my return. As of now my soul cries out to know YOU intimately. I want to laugh with Him uncontrollably. I want to write poetry for Him, read it to Him with an eager heart. I want to slow dance with Him. I want Him to become so real to me I can't wipe the grin off my face because I am so smitten by Him.

Honestly I cannot even say God will send a man to pursue my hand in marriage again. And I need to be okay with this. Once we all can get to a place where our fullness of joy comes from the pleasures of God, we begin walking with a confidence that radiates the peace and joy of Christ. We now get to use this pilgrimage as a walking example of the grace God pours down on each and everyone of us that faithfully seeks to know God.

"If it seems slow, wait for it; it will surely come; it will not delay." (Hab 2:3)

Jesus is enough. When my heart or mind wanders away toward thoughts of man rather from the richness of Jesus, I confidently say; Jesus IS enough. It seems many Christian single women or women coming out of divorce say they want a man that serves the Lord, but are not themselves being dedicated to His truths, seeking His word day in and day out, and praying on every occasion. If we want a man that is bold in sharing his faith, we need to be bold as well. If there is any ounce of us holding back, may today we take a stand for what we believe in and confidently proclaim who saved us. If we want a man that will pull us in close at night to pray for the nations, because of his love for you and the burden he has for the lost, then we must pray like that now. If we want a man that is worth waiting for, we must not let our emotions be tied to any man that rejects God, sets us up for corruption or compromise, and who can slowly pollute our mind. If you desire to be pursued and sought out, you must wait and trust the Lord to give you the desires of your heart.

> *"Look at that man, bloated by self-importance—*
> *full of himself but soul-empty.*
> *But the person in right standing before God*
> *through loyal and steady believing*
> *is fully alive, really alive." (Hab 2:4 The Message)*

There will be no doubt in your soul when this man comes along, because his loyalty to the Lord, boldness He proclaims, selfless spirit, and the way he comes after you with gentleness and confidence in the Lords calling.

Always seek the Spirit first. Pray. Reach out to your closest sister/brothers in Christ. And then wait. You deserve all you desire; but it is up to you to wait for every ounce of him.

"For God is working in you, giving you the desire and the power to do what pleases him." (Philippians 2:13)

The Spirit roared like a lion and said but you were created to desire far beyond a little hello on the other end of the phone, a second take from a guy across the room, that wonder if a text will ding, or whatever our pathetic flesh craves. I did not say you are pathetic, I said **our flesh craves the tangible**, but our Spirit longs to please God and to know Him on a more deep and intimate level.

"My soul yearns for you in the night; my spirit within me earnestly seeks you." (Isaiah 26:9)

Sweet dreams to the lonely hearted, may the warmth of the Father comfort you this night while you drift off to sleep. I am praying for the Spirit to fill your room with this prayer...."O Lord, we wait for you; your name and remembrance are the desire of our soul." (Isaiah 26:8) May your soul be so infatuated with the longing of the return of Jesus, nothing of this world taints your mind with thoughts of despair. This mystery of Christ in you, is the hope of glory. (Colossians 1:27) **Let His presence be your assurance that good things come to those who wait on the Lord.**

The role of Gods Word is to feed faith's appetite for God. And, in doing this, it WEANS my HEART away from the deceptive taste of LUST. –John Piper

The more we train our mind and heart to the living and active Word of God the stronger and wiser we become in moments of weakness. We must choose life. And this life begins by soaking in the richness of the penetrating Word of God.

When we are called to obedience we are not called just to benefit for our own good. The will of God is at stake to bless many others in ways we have no way of seeing nor understanding. **Understanding Gods ways is not the point, living out what He calls us to do is.**

Whomever or whatever is stealing precious time with the will God has for your life right now needs to go. It'll fade and flare from here and there, but it does not mean it's for the best. **Stay clear from ones that are not in it for the whole package of you.** You deserve the best.

So teach us to number our days, that we may present to you a heart of wisdom." (Psalm 90:12 NASB)

There is so much wisdom in waiting for your yoke. When you let yourself become unyoked with an unbeliever it is easy to forget who you represent. Your identity becomes theirs, because you were created to serve and help your mate. Maybe you have not tasted the richness of a God-fearing man; but WHEN you do there will be no more going back to the bars, the prowl will end, and the light will come on. His light will surround your heart, snatch it and remind you—this is what you were created for. You were created to be a light that shines so bright it makes the darkness run from you, but the ones that live for the light will want to come together with you and be even brighter as one.

You were created for fellowship not surface conversation.
You were created for intimacy not lust.

You were created for a lifelong commitment not a one-night thrill.
You were created to serve and to be served in return.

The darkness can try to be your sweet conversation, but it will fade and not blossom to what your soul truly desires and deserves.

The darkness can try and satisfy your fleshly arousals, but eventually it will not be seen as a gift but as something to be tossed to the waste can when tired of the routine. The spirit within will become stirred up. Light and darkness cannot be in the same room.

This is the kind of fast day I'm after:
to break the chains of injustice,
get rid of exploitation in the workplace,
free the oppressed,
cancel debts.

What I'm interested in seeing you do is; being available to your own families.

Do this and the lights will turn on, and your lives will turn around at once.
Your righteousness will pave your way.

I will always show you where to go.
Ill give you a full life in the emptiest of place.

You'll use the old rubble of past lives to build anew,
Rebuild the foundations from out of your past.
You'll be known as those who can fix anything,
Restore old ruins, rebuild and renovate,
Make the community livable again.

> *Then you'll be free to enjoy God!*
> *Oh, I'll make you ride high and soar above it all.*
> *I'll make you **feast** on the inheritance of your ancestor Jacob."*
> *Yes! God says so!*
> *Isaiah 58 (The MSG)*

Here I sit one day before my year commitment with a heart of tension, anger is bubbling under my skin raring to be released. I cry out for God to provide for the unexpected finances from last years taxes. I cry out for Him to show me how I am to use my gifts and provide for my children. And I cry out for Him to provide a man to walk alongside of me in pursuit of a life worshipping the Lord.

Rather I sit here with much strife within; like a time bomb about to explode. I desire to be joyful. I desire to trust Him and rejoice in the uncertainty. But joy is no where to be found. As I got on my knees this morning and gritted my teeth all I could do was just ask and hope to receive. There was no praising Him for all He had done for me this past year, but rather just expecting Him to show up. I heard Him tell me to fast and pray for these hindrances that are stealing my joy. I will fast until I feel His Peace and Joy enter my soul. I need to replace these flesh fed feelings of agitation with a hunger that relies on the true source of satisfaction.

We want Him to show up when we are fed up with waiting.
He wants us to lay it down at His feet so He can pour down a feast over our weary souls.

Purity— It is respected and desirable

"But if I say, "I will not mention his word or speak anymore in his name," his word is in my heart like a fire, a fire shut up in my bones. I am weary of holding it in; indeed, I cannot."
(Jeremiah 20:9)

This fire that burns within my soul for God I breathe in and know it is real, it is unconditional, it is pursuing me, it is speaking to me, it is alive, and it penetrates me to a life of thankfulness, freedom, confidence and joy.

The fire that burned within my body for sex I wanted to hide and run to it when it was dark. I did not want the emotions to get too close; but how naïve when it was the closest you can become with another individual. I wanted more, but deep down I knew it would die out. I had disconnected and let numbness be my safeguard. This numbness was representing death. *"Then, after desire has conceived, it gives birth to sin; and sin, when it is full-grown, gives birth to death." (James 1:15)*

There is a difference between these two fires.

The fire that burns for God is sustaining, satisfying, sanctifying, and gives me strength. It brings trembling and fear as I picture in my mind.... *"But small is the gate and narrow the road that leads to life, and only a few find it."* (Matthew 7:14)

The fire that burned for man was leading me to death, not life. It took me to darkness, defeat, depression, and despair.

We are not capable of tweaking Gods plan for our lives rather He interrupts ours. If He has called us to a life of obedience, He will not let us go and wander away too far. Once you taste the grace of God there is nothing more that can ever truly satisfy.

Sweet Jesus keep us on track. Keep distractions away from our sight. And if another piece of bait is thrown in front of us, give us the strength to fight it, as we know the end result will be to run back to you; and another piece of our heart will be given away where it did not need to be given.

> *"For the spirit of whoredom is within them, and they know not the Lord." (Hosea 5:4)*

Can I even write what I want to reveal about my "whoredom?" If I am honest, will it set me free? The song. *"If were honest"* comes to mind and speaks to my issue this day, and the story I want to tell to all that read my journey. Is it a fun one? No. Is it a lighthearted and joyful journey? No. Is it full of success stories? Nope. Is it a journey filled with brokenness? Yes. It is a story that brings to the table grace after grace after grace when I return right back where I began.

Francesca Battistelli sings...

> *"truth is harder than a lie, the dark seems safer than the light...and everyone has a heart that loves to hide, I'm a mess and so are you. We've built walls that nobody can get through. yeah, it may be hard, but the best thing we could*

*ever do. **bring your brokenness, and I'll bring mine**."*

She sings on about being honest with ourselves and being honest with others. And it will change our lives, and set us free. **Confessing your greatest weakness will turn into your greatest strength**. I love how God orchestrates ashes to beauty.

Not one vision comes to mind where I feel fulfilled, desired, respected, or loved when I sought out selfishly gratifying my desires. I wonder how many people would say they are struggling with this right now. I can honestly look back on these pathetic nightly endeavors and say I am freed of my sexual gratifications for a life of eternal satisfaction being the stronger desire. I made a public confession to two elders in church one morning. I wept after not crying for a year. I released it for a greater gain; the true satisfaction of the Heavenly King.
We are not capable of tweaking Gods plan for our lives rather He interrupts our measly plans for a greater purpose. It took a couple years but I now see how God asked me in July 2014 to give Him my full heart and dedication to reveal to me, THIS was my weakness. And this weakness revealed my lack of trust, disrespect for myself, and a disconnected awareness of my worth. He used the most tainted mysterious gift to man and woman because it is intended for a connection that can represent the beauty of our King with the church. He will let us taste death so we can truly begin living.

Deep down there is a groaning stirring within, you may not be coherent enough to let it wake you. I assure you that brokenness is wanting to set you free. God wants all of you, and He will let us wander and taste death if it takes getting us to return to His safe-haven. This journey of breaking free takes way more than just a desire to want to change, however that is a good starting place. But it also takes a full blown out action of repentance. When we can admit our weakness without letting the shame of it defeat us into hibernation, we must take this time of courage and run with it toward the Cross.

Forgive Yourself

I have been reminded this morning even after the past couple days of feeling distant from the Lord, and waking to a surprising and strange dream of my x husband kissing me... God sent me two messages through two different women ...God told me, I am for you and I am fighting for you. I love when God ties visions I had the day before, with a sister in Christ words today together. I do not believe things just randomly happen; but know without a doubt when we submit to His voice and do not get in the way, beautiful pictures unfold.

Yesterday as my kids and I were running around at a park we go to regularly; I was stopped in my tracks when I looked down at a patch of sandy dirt. I was taken back to the story of Jesus and the woman caught in adultery. The anger and insults that raged all around her, and how grace was no where to be found. However in our darkest hours Jesus still shows up, and not only did He set the accusers in their place, He granted much tender love to the one caught in adultery. How humiliated she must have felt. Jesus chose to write in the dirt where it probably left His hands stained with a residue of mud. As He stood back up He did not shove His dirty hands in her face and call her degrading words, but rather He demonstrated why He came to this earth. He came to clean us from our impure thoughts and actions. He demonstrated how to show grace to ones caught in sin. He demonstrated love.

The sun was setting through the trees and glistening over this sand, and I could not help to relive it and draw a line in the sand that separated the accusers from the woman and Jesus. And I still wonder what Jesus wrote in the sand, simply I think just as he asked Adam and Eve *"where are you"* even when He knew...He simply wrote... *"WHO"*

*"Let any one of you **who** is without sin be the first to throw a stone at her." (John 8:7)*

I saw people watching me as I was reliving this moment; but I never want to miss a moment with God, as if I did not do this yesterday, todays word crazy enough came from a quote of the man that actually married my x and me... and my heart aches. But as Dr. Tom Hufty asked my dear friend during her time of grief after divorce, it speaks to me just as boldly...

"God does not care if the vessel is chipped or cracked, only if it's clean. Are you clean?"

YOU HAVE BEEN REDEEMED TO GO AND SHARE WHAT GOD HAS RESTORED IN YOUR LIFE!

Once you are so content in waiting for the desires God has placed in your heart, wait for them in holy surrender so you can get back to completely focusing on the gifts that have been given to you THIS day---your children.

CHILDREN-They Need You

"Love the Lord your God with all your heart and with all your soul and with all your strength. These commandments that I give you today are to be on your hearts. **Impress them on your children"** *(Deut 6:4-7)*

Our kitchen is for dancing.

And the LORD will guide you continually and satisfy your desire in scorched places and make your bones strong; and you shall be like a watered garden, like a spring of water, whose waters do not fail" (Isaiah 58:11)

I hate winter. It was my lowest of time the first year after my x and I split, and I had set in my mind and heart it would not defeat me the following. But, one evening in the winter of 2015 I found myself on my couch for 2 hours after my kids left to go to their dads, not able to get up. And as the sun set and it got darker, and then the death hour of pitch black caved in. It was as if I began drifting off to a world of lies, pain, and felt there was no one close. I became completely nauseous and the thought of food made me want to vomit. I share this because you need to know you are not alone.

You are not alone in your doubts about the existence of God in your lowest moments. As I have struggled with this from time to time in the past couple months. You are not alone in the craziest thoughts you have imagined. But the steadfastness of Gods unfailing love never ceases to amaze me when His Spirit groans within me and prays for me, and gets me to His Word for strength, a phone call to my parents, a text to a good friend to pray for me. And when all those lies are lifted and I am at complete peace, I quickly am reminded I am not alone. I am being held. I am being healed. It is okay to doubt but I assure you there is a brighter day coming.

This past week I have found myself getting on my knees whenever a free moment was presented. Both children were happily playing, and my heart was burning deep inside to be in communion with God. I quietly walked to my room, because they love being in the same room with me at all times even if we are not talking (hmmm, wonder who they get that from) ;) I dropped to my knees at my bed, and laid my head down and began releasing my heartaches to God and my desire to love Him with all my heart. It was not only 2 minutes until I hear my door open, and it was such a sweet moment as instead of my daughter asking what I was doing, as she knew, she just laid on my back and held onto me as I sought the Lord. The Lord is our Comfort. Wait for it. He will come. He will show up when we least expect it. And this is how I want my children to remember me. Seeking the Lord.

"As for me and my house, we will serve the Lord." (Joshua 24:15)

When was the last time you let your walls down in front of your children? It is okay to be raw with them as they already discern more than we give them credit. A beautiful bond that uniquely happens is when we let our children see the floodgates open with tears. **God gave us the power to cry to release sorrow**. I am not encouraging uncontrollably crying that your children do not feel safe, but tears that show a sincere pain. If we stuff or hide our pain our children will too. What better time to show them it is okay to shed tears and discuss the matter rather crying, drinking, and inviting men over. Your children need ALL of you.

My daughter caught me sniffling in the kitchen and we just held one another; as today she cried she didn't want to be away from me. But I'm reminded our tears are not meaningless... And that my tears have been put in a bottle, and God has recorded our wanderings. (Ps 56:8-9) Tomorrow will be a new day of blessings, as today was a day of quietness and

freeing the walls inside me that needed to be released. God hates divorce but He always brings good out of any situation.

> *"If I must boast, I will boast of the things that show my weakness." (2 Corinthians 11:30)*

I want to be confident in my weaknesses to show the strength of where God has brought me from. I do not want to hide my fears, my failures, and weaknesses from anyone. And when I say anyone, most importantly my children. Just last night I was asked by a dear friend—what about when one day your kids read your book and read of your wanderings. I have thought about this multiple times, and even while writing the words I use I am cautious with because one day my kids or friends kids will see what I have written and where I have been on this pilgrimage. If I shrink back from what the Lord has told me I am not living out His calling nor the power of His word. *"For God has not given us a spirit of fear and timidity, but of power, love, and self-discipline."* (2 Timothy 1:7)

No matter the voyage you choose to take, once we let God be our everything we are to *tell the world how he freed us from oppression*. (Psalm 107:2) The MSG

I much rather my children know their mother as one that is honest with her weaknesses, and that life is not about masking who we truly are and where we have come from. And one day I look forward to sitting down and having a heart to heart with my children, but until that day I want to write them a letter/poem that will go in their journals. And look forward to the day they open this entry as it will be smothered in prayer for the Lord to speak to their hearts and draw them close to Him.

Dearest child of mine,
You have been with me since the womb.
You have seen me cry, you have seen me hold my head high.
You have seen our family of 4 go to a family of 3 in just your few short years of life.
Mommy is so proud of you, because I see you walk with confidence. And I see your eyes sparkle with delight. You are dearly loved. You are cherished. And it makes momma proud you know you are so very loved.
You have asked if friends of yours parents live in different homes. You are no fool, you are quite aware of your surroundings.
You laugh when you hurt, and I hurt when I know the laugh. But mommy wants you to know God is not finished with us yet.

Our home may not look like the rest, but it does not mean this is not Gods best.
The best may yet still to come.
All I know is to show you that through the brokenness God has given me the strength. God has given me grace. God has showered down His love on me each and every day.
"His going out is sure as the dawn; He will come to us as the showers, as the spring rains that water the earth." (Hosea 6:3)

Mommy has dedicated her life to the steadfast love of God. Where I seek to be swooned by God and not man.
I see the hunger in your eyes for the complete picture of a daddy and mommy. I see how you look at daddies when it's the 3 of us.
The prayer that resides within to come alive in your soul.... *"He will cover you with his feathers. He will shelter you with his*

wings. His faithful promises are your armor and protection."
(Psalm 91:4)

On days you catch mommy sniffling in the kitchen or in my bedroom, do know these tears are not meaningless. These tears have shaped me. These tears are healing me. These tears I want to share with you; because you are a part of me. These tears are not defeating me; they are giving me strength and wisdom.

When I wake each morning I can not wait to serve you. I can not wait to pray with you. I can not wait to have you follow me to every room. I can not wait to laugh with you. I can not wait to brush you hair. I can not wait to send you off to school to be a light to all you come in contact with.

I am going to mess up today. I will get impatient. Ill probably look at my phone too many times. And I am sorry, and I pray we will always be a family that says sorry when we know we have failed one another. I am sorry you have to share your parents in different homes. I am sorry when I hurt inside and I become irritable.
The love I have for you will only grow stronger. I am always here for you. And I will never leave you. You are my precious gift God gave me to nurture and raise you to know the gospel. I pray in my motherhood each day I live out the gospel, and you remember me as a woman that feared the Lord and trusted the Lord with all my heart, soul, and mind.

I love you sweet child of mine,
Momma

Whatever strength you can muster up this day, whatever convictions, heart ache you can't express to your children face to face, the sorrow it brings to you that your children live in a broken home go get it down on paper. And on a day you feel ready to hand it to them, give it to them with victory in your eyes. Tell them how God set you free. No child condemns a parent that is raw and honest in love with them. But I can assure you, they want to see you smile again, laugh with them so hard it hurts, see confidence when you walk, and hear you give God all the glory and praise. Be the example they deserve. Be the assurance to them that your broken home does not make them nor you as a family damaged. Pilgrim, remember we are just passing through, and they are the next generation that will carry on the legacy of faith you choose to leave them.

"Let us then with confidence draw near to the throne of grace, that we may receive mercy and find grace to help in time of need." (Hebrews 4:16)

When we are able to stop comparing our home to others we then are able to accept our own "normal" is beautiful too. We have to embrace our lifestyles with grace and make the most of each day. I really can't imagine my life any different now as a family of 3....after much denial, anger, and depression...but now this is us and I wouldn't have it any other way even if it

isn't the "norm."

Masking our rooted pain surfaces at the most random times. Search it out. Talk it out with a dear friend. Regret. Shattered dreams. Old anniversary dates that no longer exist. Still loving your x. These are all normal tucked away sorrows that will take daily healing. You deserve to laugh again and to be dined and wined. And when you do, don't race to future thoughts. Focus on today's scars. Today's joys. Today's walls. Rest in where you are today. I can not encourage being still and resting enough. My resting place has become my back patio where I light up a fire and listen to it crackle and pop. I know I am not alone. You are not alone. God does not ask for perfection. He simply just asks you to obey and trust Him. This is your time for refining. Keep investing in your closest friends. Keep letting your closest friends love you. You are stronger today whether you believe it or not.

"For I have given you an example, that you also should do just as I have done to you."(John 13:15)

      The first gift under the tree was to my children's daddy the second year after we separated. I found much joy taking my kids today to pick out a gift for the man they love. They deserve to be able to enjoy the blessing of giving, and there is no reason for me to keep that from them. The worst thing a divorced or separated parent can do for their children is to talk down of the other parent. No matter how bad the situation. Because to children all they know is the love they have for the parent that once use to live with them. **It is our responsibility to teach our children grace and how to live it out.** I honestly did not have to grit my teeth while doing this today because knowing the joy it brought to my kids to partake in gift giving. Life may not seem fair to us adults as our dream of marriage ended, but there's no excuse to take joy from our children because we hurt. Please hear my sincere request that our children need us to teach them how to walk in love. There will be times for us to vent and scream about our once partner, but, there is no pardon for that in front of the children we created with that person. They deserve more that that.

What do your children need from you most?

But grace was given to each one of us according to the measure of Christ's gift. (Ephesians 4:7)

What a beautiful picture of the gospel I witnessed this morning. My daughter gave the gift with fervent delight; and then it was received with surprise and humble thankfulness. This reminded me of the eagerness God has when He knocks on our door to give us the gift of freedom. He smiles. He can't wait for us to open it. He can't wait for us to be part of His family.

We never will experience the joy God wants us to embrace if we don't move forward in grace.

"Indeed, we felt that we had received the sentence of death. But that was to make us rely not on ourselves but on God who raises the dead." (2 Cor 1:9)

There will be days of anguish that will grip your heart so tight but will have to stand so brave. As the words of my son are ringing in my ears as I buckled him in his car seat to go to his dads. *"momma, can you please come with us."* And one week from today we will begin the week to week schedule. I can not bare the thought of what I will miss out on when they are gone in the evenings. What funny stories they will tell, when they fall and need to be held, when they are running a high fever and I am not there to serve them, massage them, give them a warm bubble bath with relaxing music on, discipline them when needing correction, wiping their tears off their face, snuggling them because they are my children that I birthed into this world. The 9 months I held them in my womb to now only getting to be part of their lives half of the time. Tears are streaming down my face so heavily I can barely breathe, and all I want is to hold my babies right now. There will be days like this. *"There is no wisdom, no insight; no plan that can succeed against the Lord."* (Proverbs 21:30) Divorce is of man not of God. No matter who chose to pull the plug and get a divorce their plan will not rise above the Lords blueprint for your life.

Squeeze your child an extra time today, look them in the eye and tell them you're proud to call them your child, smile at them across the room, make loud fart noises and laugh until it hurts, build forts and play in it with them, be the first to say your sorry, when they accidently make a mess let them know accidents happen, and they can easily be cleaned up. Make the aroma of your love be so close to them even when your away from them that when they close their eyes they see your face. Because one day these spinning out of control days will not be at our fingertips. They are our responsibility. Love them well. And give a kiss to your child right now for me, will ya? Your child is destined to be the change in our generation of divorce.

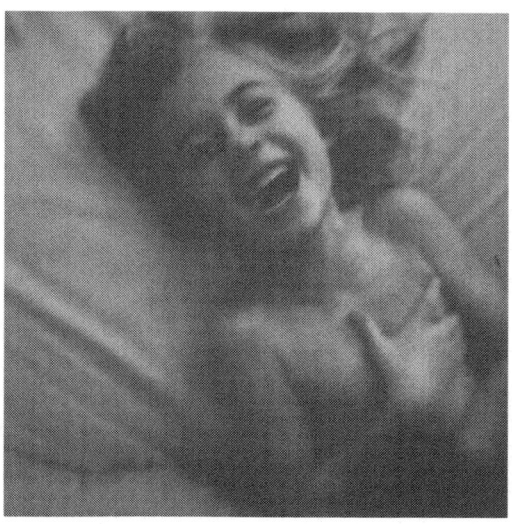

I could barely walk out of my daughter's room tonight as I knew it was the last night to put her to bed until next week. I gave her a massage tonight with some yummy lavender oils, we giggled, sang the songs I have been singing to her every night since she embraced my arms, we prayed, and then I held her so close. I move once, and she will always ask for two more minutes. But tonight, I let those two minutes turn into 30 minutes. I just breathed in her smell, stared at her long lashes, big lips, round cheeks, and listened to her breath get louder as she drifted off to sleep. As I slipped out of her bed, I could not help but to tell her how beautiful she was, and then I told her how proud I was of her. I walked toward the door, turned around to say I love you one more time, then to only go back to her bed and kiss her a few more times. I could not help but well up with tears.

I trust my daughter knows she is loved in action and words. I trust this pilgrimage is not by accident, but by choice. The last thing I whispered to Abigail tonight was…. "you are going to touch so many peoples lives one day."

God is educating you; that's why you must never drop out. He's treating you as dear children. This trouble you're in isn't punishment; it's training, the normal experience of children. Only irresponsible parents leave children to fend for themselves. Would you prefer an irresponsible God? We respect our own parents for training and not spoiling us, so why not embrace God's training so we can truly live? While we were children, our parents did what seemed best to them. But God is doing what is best for us, training us to live God's holy best. At the time, discipline isn't much fun. It always feels like it's going against the grain. Later, of course, it pays off handsomely, for it's the well-trained who find themselves mature in their relationship with God. (Heb 12:7-11 The MSG)

They need us. They need our assurance. They need our laughter. They need our dedication. They need our discipline. They need to enjoy their childhood. They may not be living the dream of two parents in one home but remember you are not alone and you can do it with the strength of Jesus.
Yesterday my daughter said randomly and innocently. *"Momma, I follow you. I do what you do."* How simple, but how profound. She is watching me. She is studying me. She is following my lead. It gave me that much more encouragement to not bring a man into my life for my pleasure. However she desires for me to have a boyfriend. The innocence of a child wants what they were created for. This always gives me the opportunity to share with my children how I am trusting the Lords lead and will when it comes to dating. It gives me the opportunity to live out my faith in front of them and for them to see me rely on the Lord as my strength and satisfaction. One day my children will grow up and will want to venture into the dating scene or begin having crushes. As my daughter said, she is following my lead and doing as I do. I want her to follow in the footsteps the Lord is leading me to live out.
  As my children came first. They get me first. All of me. I will continue to follow the lead of Christ in these convictions as I have two children to train up to be world changers for Christ.

For where two or three are gathered in my name, there am I among them. (Matthew 18:20) (ESV)

Last year this time I was chasing after darkness; empty sources of life. I was so consumed with feeding my flesh, there was no room in my heart for light.
It is no coincidence that this beautiful metaphor was given to me as my children and I chased after lightning bugs last night. As we were pulling into our driveway; my son squealed as he saw one light up in our yard. My kids had already unbuckled their seatbelts, hands on the door handle, waiting for me to park so they could sprint to those beautiful creatures of light. We all ran with giddiness, jumping, chasing, squealing everytime we saw one.

It was not until I was laying in bed; exhausted, but heart so full. I was reminded of the responsibility of raising my two children to be chasers of the light. Yesterday afternoon I invited my children to pray with me, of course they asked why. Which I was then able to share with them when two or three are gathered in Jesus name, there He is among us—and there is more power in numbers. If you are a single mom—I pray you are able to see your children as world changers. They need us to be faithful chasers of light before them, to know how to follow His lead. Our world desperately needs us to be people that let the light of Jesus shine. The people of this age need world changers that bring light, hope, and joy. And it all starts with us. It starts with you.

It started when you came to grips with admitting your helplessness. God has you right where He wants you. No more aimlessly running to empty wells but to a life toward living out the gifts of faith, hope, and love.

FAITH

"Beloved, I urge you as sojourners and exiles to abstain from the passions of the flesh, which wage war against your soul."
(1 Peter 2:11 ESV)

Seeking to live a life of contentment in a world where war is raging against anything lovely and pure is the biggest step of faith I have ever taken. However, I can sit here and answer my own question—"has there ever been any good outcome when I held onto a certain pleasure of the world?" The only outcome that came was a slow death to my soul, where I could no longer live in freedom, but became a slave to my master of sin. A good way to test if you are a slave— is when you bow down and respond when sin knocks on the door of your inner desires and thoughts. There is a difference when God knocks on the door and sin knocks. God does not bring turmoil within; He brings peace.

How does one live a life of contentment when war is raging within? There is always an answer of hope when we look to His Word. Philippians 4:8 reminds us.... *"Finally, brothers, whatever is TRUE, whatever is HONORABLE, whatever is JUST, whatever is PURE, whatever is LOVELY, whatever is COMMENDABLE, if there is any excellence, if there is anything worthy of praise, think about these things."* If you are like me and are fed up with this restlessness within, you are ready to take this step of faith with me. He knows when we are ready to walk by faith. When tests come to keep us moving forward you must trust His lead and let Him take care of your doubts. Even after 2 years of breaking strongholds the tests do not end. This does not sound assuring does it; but really it is quite the opposite. God has no intension of leading you to a place of courage and confidence to not put your strength to the test from a different angle. Take courage He sees a strength in you your not aware of quite yet. He is about to reveal your ultimate testimony. When others are saying I just don't understand why she keeps getting hit from every angle, maybe that very person needed to see faith lived out when you kept getting back up and striving onward to a life of victory. My faith awakening happened 2 years later when strongholds had been released, confidence in God over man became my satisfaction, and I know longer was running to quick fixes.

After a long dreary day of non-stop rain, $75 in my checking account, encountering a still and quiet mood, but much a full trust in My Provider and Comforter. And yes a distant aching over my divorce. The Lord spoke after 2 days of silence... He does this you know? He not only tells us to be still to not move; but to wait for His lead. He longs for our pursuit of Him. I listened. Joy rang inside my soul. What He revealed only makes sense now because of all the trials He has put me through. If He shared this word with me a year ago I would not have been ready for it. His anointed timing is always the sweetest. Gods pace is never rushed. It is natural and not forced. This time my heart was ready to hear Him say, take courage when facing trials, it is His way of reminding us we are not to get too comfortable here. We are just passing through. Trials become our testimony! <u>Stay uprooted, so **when** the next trial comes you will not be attached but free and ready to move onward with the Lords plan for your life.</u>

God uproots us because He demands us to not get comfortable here. We are not just pilgrims passing through, but beautiful warrior pilgrims getting to leave a legacy of faith to the next generation of believers. When we face a trial or the biggest storm its because we were trying to get too comfortable here, he is reminding us we do not live for this world. So let us stop clinging to the things of this world, to the trinkets and gifts to this world. But rather give our life, heart, and things to God.

We are on a voyage.

Your lack of comfort is the first step to walking freely.

"Yet even now," declares the LORD, "return to me with all your heart, with fasting, with weeping, and with mourning." (Joel 2:12)

A day will come when your living life with your children in a way you could never imagine it not ever being. One day we were outside breathing in the fresh air, making forts out of our dead sunflower stems from last summers garden, cutting down an overgrown butterfly bush, made a fire to keep away the brisk breeze, soaking in the view of my kids using their imagination, and humbled by how close they wanted to be as I cleaned up in our back yard.

Have you caught onto the theme yet? That reminder from God for us to repent, be alert and **return with ALL our heart**. How many times does He have to draw us back? What life or death situation will He have to use to get our attention once again? How long will we stay in comfort rather than putting out a fire as quickly as possible before it destroys everything you have worked for, loved, and watch grow from the ground up?

Yesterday if you could have seen me in action after my son came into the home in a panic. All he could say was, "momma I didn't mean to, come outside..." I never imagined to see our grass spreading in a wildfire. Thankful we had a hose hooked up and close by. I was in sheer panic inside, but I had to focus and react quickly, as some of the fire was up against our home, and heading toward our wooden fence.

God is waiting to activate what He already planned to do. He wants us to understand being ready for action is living out your faith. But, while in the fire of testing is when we have to focus, put our game faces on and put out whatever is hindering our journey of faith. So, have you been put through the testing's of the fire? Are you ready to take action with this pain you are facing? What is holding you back from adjusting to a lifestyle of concentration toward the One that is waiting for you to return? Or maybe you are not in a place of needing to return, but time to take the leap of faith to hold onto His hope He paved the way for us to follow in all seasons of our lives.

Putting out a fire gives no space for comfort. It takes action. However, I understand healing takes time. And once the fire is put out, there is still much damage to the visible eye. **The stain of the pain takes time to slowly fade**. One turn of the head and you see it in plain sight. It takes time to come back to life. It will take fertilizing. It will take tender care to bring back to lush color again. As we lose that glow when our life shatters, it will come back after consistent focus on nourishing our soul with meat that will make us full and not search in empty dark places that only cut us off from growth and new life.

But my life is worth nothing to me unless I use it for finishing the work assigned me by the Lord Jesus--the work of telling others the Good News about the wonderful grace of God.
(Acts 20:24) NLT

Have you noticed in your time of suffering and refining, non-believers have come into your life, or maybe been there all along but are more aware of the rejection to the One that has carried you through your thickest storm?

The Son of God suffered unto the death,
Not that men might not suffer, but that their
Sufferings might be like His.
George Macdonald

This taste of poison we have experienced has been gifted to our hearts to live on with purpose. The flu-like achiness that touches you from your head to your toes will only be temporary. When Jesus uttered His last words, "It is finished", He know longer felt the spear that pierced His side,

the gaping open wounds burn from the dirt, spit, and sweat that absorbed into His mangled flesh.
His suffering we will never be able to taste and feel as He did, but through His Word and Spirit we can pass on His testimony; the gift of salvation. Last night before I went to sleep, I was being pulled back to dig deeper into the story of the Samaritan woman. As I refuse to let the fear of people hold me back from sharing the transformation God has done in my life.

"MANY Samaritans from the town believed in him because of the woman's testimony." (John 4:39)

He will use ones to share on His testimony that have been through the fire, have tasted darkness, but in the end was healed by the power and love of Jesus.

I wonder how many times the Samaritan woman caught herself saying, "I rushed into another love affair, a fantasy that did not quench the thirst I was searching for; longing for." But once touched by the living water she could not keep it to herself. It had to be shared because it was by far the sweetest embrace she had ever experienced. And for the first time she rushed to tell everyone of this living water that did not leave her parched for more. She ran to tell everyone she knew, with no shame of who she may have been known as in the town. I am sure there were some that whispered, and did not give her an ear. **Her act of obedience outweighed the shame she had carried for too long.** No longer did she walk in condemnation, but freedom to share of the good news of eternal water that never goes dry. Freedom—that is what Jesus offers.

"IF you'll hold on to me for dear life, says God, I'll get you out of any trouble." (Psalm 91:14) The Message

Balancing good in my life has never come easy to me. I'm either black or white, all or nothing, or dead set on one passion. As I have been crying out to God this morning over

Psalm 91, verse 14 put me in a dead hault to lift my hands to the Lord and cry out in anguish and passion that I would hold onto to Him so tight as I would on the Ninja at Six Flags. As I hold on for dear life I am frightened but secure in the harnesses from despair. I get jolted to the left then to the right, my stomach turns, and I can barely see straight; but as I am still holding on for dear life, the ride keeps moving forward, never back to the beginning to start all over again. A few moments we get to catch our breath, look at the top of the mountain and remember all the beauty that is still around us to enjoy, but its in that very moment we have to choose—will we grasp for the world to hold us tight at night, during moments of weakness in the day. Or will we hold on for dear life to finish the race that God has right before us. The test will come even when the ride comes to a slower pace, this is when we have to close our eyes, take another deep breath and choose to let God hold us all the way to the finish line.

Even so faith, if it has no works, is dead, being by itself.
(James 2:17)

Weary soul? Be patient with yourself. Don't rush. Do not try and understand the lack of life within. There has never been a storm that has lasted a lifetime. Faith is your best friend right now; rely on it even when there is not an ounce of joy within. Self-examination is a must each day. What have you examined about yourself today?

The further we get away from His Word, the further we get from living out a life of discipline. And the further discipline slips from our grasp, the further we get from living a life of faith. The more we rely on our emotions, the further we get from a life of peace. You are going to desire what you put your most focus on.

"The place where your treasure is, is the place you will most want to be, and end up being." (Matthew 6 The Msg)

And this desire you have may not be bad, but when it becomes a distraction, a consuming passion, and leads you to confusion, you must ask yourself, what is the Spirit revealing to you? *"Give your entire attention to what God is doing right now, and don't get worked up about what may or may not happen tomorrow. God will help you deal with whatever hard things come up when the time comes." (Matthew 6 The MSG)*

If you remain in Me and My words remain in you, ask whatever you want and it will be done for you. (John 15:7)

There is that big word IF once again. If we trust will we obey, and if we obey will we trust? We cannot have one without the other and truly dwell with Jesus. **Fear is what holds one back from accepting the gift of freedom**. If we can learn to remain in Christ we must first trust in Him with all our heart, soul, and mind. Trust Him to heal your heart. Trust Him to satisfy your soul. Trust Him to guide your thoughts.

How determined are you to committing a lifestyle of vigorous attention on the alluring Spirit that is calling you to Himself? The time is now, today. Our yesterday is history; did you leave a legacy? Our tomorrow is already paved for you; so do not fret. But this beautiful today is more than just a cup of coffee to get your blood a pumping. Today is serious business, serious obedience; this life you have been given is not to be abused and taken for granted. You have a serious calling on your life, in the name of Jesus. Breathe it in and believe it; and it will be granted to you. When you are ready to live for the One that created your heart for His worship, watch your desires wildly change to what He desires. **Wildly pursue the One that created your heart on this gifted pilgrimage.**

"Bless the Lord, O my soul, and all that is within me, bless his holy name!" (Psalm 103:1

There is much the observer does not feel nor understand personally while watching what these group of girls are bearing. One of the girls mentioned how they never knew when one girl was going to move and adjust the weight, and then had to focus and find balance all over again. But the whole time there was a group of friends there still holding the weight when one was having to shift and still move forward. Divorce looks and feels a lot like this. The heaviness at times seems unbearable to hold; but with the right support group walking alongside you, they will not let you do it alone. When we let go and truly put our faith in our Protector, the pain will still come, but not defeat us any longer. It is okay to feel the pain; as this pain will stretch those faith muscles. If we do not stretch in our faith, we will only shrink. You have come too far to start shrinking back now. Keep moving forward to the living water, hand over that weight you are no longer required to bear alone.
The Lord says…. "Come, everyone who thirsts, come to the water." (Isaiah 55: 1)

Confident of your obedience, I write to you, knowing that you will do even more than I ask. (Phil. 1:21)

When my daughter was 6 she ran her first one mile race. She had no idea what to expect, besides; just run. She knew that at the end there would be a reward, a ribbon that proved she finished. When they said, on your mark, get set, GO her legs started moving forward, and she was focused. She gave me a glance on the sidelines, but her task in front of her was what she needed to concentrate on. Because if she decided to blow me kisses, run backwards until she couldn't see me any longer, lets be honest she would have fallen and busted her tail bottom in no time. Rather, she put her game face on and went for it.
 No one can finish the race for you, even when your biggest fans are on the sidelines cheering you on. **We are solely responsible for our race.** But, if we do not have supporters walking along our side when we want to stop because it hurts too much, we may never make it to the finish line. Who would you rather be--the one that passed out from exhaustion of trying to do it all on their own, or the one that persevered with pain and much sweat but finished the race?

"Now faith is confidence in what we hope for and assurance about what we do not see" (Hebrews 11:1) NIV

I waited in anticipation to see my blonde hair beauty return in her favorite colors, pink and purple. And when I saw her, I could not help but jog toward her, yell out her name—YAAAAY ABIGAL, YOU CAN DO IT—GO GO GO!!! She smiled at me. Tears streamed down my face. I jogged down to the finish line to see her with the ribbon in hand. I asked her, how do you feel baby girl—you did it! "Momma, not so good" ☺ But, you did it! You finished! You sprinted to the end!
That is all God asks of us. Finish the race He has set out before you. You may grit your teeth when smiling because the reward is in eye sight. And you know, if you made it thus far, there is no turning back now. He has carried you all the way even

when you did not see Him. He carried you through with your biggest fans. He carried you through with your closest friends that know your deepest darkest secrets. He carried you through with the blood that conceived you and brought you into this world.

Confidence in the One that called you out to this pilgrimage will bring you to a place where you throw your arms up in surrender. Surrender because you know there is no doubt in your soul that the only reason you made it to the finish line was because of the One that called you to a life of faith. This leap caused much tension from the unknown. The unknown was known to the One that placed the calling, and from that calling you trusted, sweat, screamed, hurt, pressed on, and simply learned to let go and trust God.

I am proud of you. I am cheering for you. You can do this. You will not be disappointed by His protection.

The more we die to the perishable enjoyments the more we will be filled with the knowledge of wisdom.
The knowledge of wisdom comes from seeking His Word, from falling on your knees every morning ready to surrender to His will. Be still and wait for the Lord. You will be full.

"The fundamental fact of existence is that this trust in God, this faith, is the firm foundation under everything that makes life worth living. Its our handle on what we cant see. The act of faith is what distinguished our ancestors, set them above the crowd." (Hebrews 11:1) The MSG

My heart yearns to not only get by and barely pass through this life that has been given to me. But to pass through as a true pioneer—focused on a life that drinks of the Spirit of God. And there is no other woman that I desire to live on my faith like Elisabeth Elliot did. This beautiful woman passed through this world with much grace. And the summer of 2015 she entered into the gates of gold. I can only imagine the rejoicing and celebration that went on. I cannot even fathom the true suffering she experienced; **but she received it and trusted it.**

"I realized that the deepest spiritual lessons are not learned by His letting us have our way in the end, but by His making us wait, bearing with us in love and patience until we are able to honestly to pray what He taught His disciples to pray: Thy will be done."

HOPE- Rest

Where can I go from your Spirit?
Where can I flee from your presence?
If I go up to the heavens, you are there;
if I make my bed in the depths, you are there.
If I rise on the wings of the dawn,
if I settle on the far side of the sea,
even there your hand will guide me,
your right hand will hold me fast. (Psalm 139:7-10)

Winter resembles a time of stillness in my soul. As winter I believe is here for us to be forced to reflect and examine our surroundings, our current circumstances, and to enjoy the slower pace of life. There are no lush green leaves waving back and forth when the wind is howling. Rather the limbs stand there bare and naked waiting to be clothed again. We can find much encouragement during our time of shedding rather than letting the winter weight pack on the wrong coverings.

Embrace the nakedness to let God take complete control of your brand new garments.

As His coverings will take root, and grow into a beautiful masterpiece that leaves you and others in awe of His beautiful pursuit.

The Proverbs 31 woman covered herself with strength and dignity. (Proverbs 31:25) She did not pack on winter weight that would bog her down, but rather let the Lord cover her in garments of caliber. "And she laughs at the time to come." V.25 I see this laughter she is portraying as confidence in the Lords provisions, merely, she also does not sit around waiting for God to move and do it all. She does not laugh out of arrogance nor laughs as a defense to being anxious within. We may not be able to compare our status as a wife with the Proverbs woman any longer, but lets take off our worldly glasses, and look through the lens of hope and a new beginning. As this season of shedding an outward role we once embraced with all our heart as a wife now gets to turn into a season of packing on the bread of life.

I could not agree more with Elisabeth Elliot's wisdom.... *"God will not protect you from anything that will make you more like Jesus."* He wants to strip us from any idleness we use to cover up embarrassment, guilt, pleasures we are hiding behind. As many winters come around for their time of shedding and nakedness; we too will come face to face with the realization God is never finished with us.
Jesus wants us to live in freedom, and we cannot arrive until we accept His water of eternal life. The pursuit of His love is shown to us in the story of the Samaritan woman. The encounter Jesus had with the Samaritan woman strikes me deep within. As it appears this woman was looking to be fulfilled by man, but after being with five that were none being her husband at the encounter, she longed to hear how she could *"not be thirsty or have to come draw water anymore."*

How many times do we want out of a situation that is not fulfilling our thirst; but only know the way back to the raging war within that wants to be fed?

The more we feed the thirst of our bodies craving, our body becomes conditioned into believing this is what keeps it alive.

This longing for more, this pursuit for satisfaction is a spiritual thirst that has been put under a bushel and no longer able to come up for air if it tried. But listen to this, today is a new day, even if you went out last night and gave your body away to someone.
This word is for you right now, the Samaritan woman never found peace within until the hushing of Jesus' truth was handed over to her. It was not until she was all alone; away from the crashing noises of war inside her body. Jesus was right where He wants us all to be with our brokenness, face to face with Him. Jesus was coming; and when He came, the

ones that held the most shame, brokenness, and filth were who He pursued. So if you are finding yourself believing you are not worthy of this everlasting water, drown that lie out with this truth…. *"The thief comes only to steal and kill and destroy. I came that they may have life and have it abundantly." (John 10:10)*

"Jesus said to her, "Everyone who drinks of this water will be thirsty again, but whoever drinks of the water that I will give him will never be thirsty again." (John 4:13) She willingly accepted and believed when given this gift of freedom. The handful of men she had given her body to never quenched her thirst, they only left her feeling she needed more to find her worth and security.

Just as the trees have no chance of changing this season, as it is inevitable, this chapter of our life is happening whether we like it or not. And also as the wintery trees are stripped of all their outward beauty, left to stand tall and reveal the intricate beauty of what is not able to be seen during the seasons of growth, we are letting go of baggage that no longer defines us. It is going back to the dust of the world. Just as the trees have lost all their leaves, we feel a stripping of our role as a helpmate. We feel exposed to the world; bitter and desperate for warmth to rise up through the roots of what once was our comfort.

The seasons that feel the most bitter are the ones that produce the most fruit.

But this fruit I speak of are the ones that take much pruning, stillness, discipline, and desire for His presence.

"Meanwhile we groan, longing to be clothed instead with our heavenly dwelling, because when we are clothed, we will not be found naked." (2 Cor. 5:2-3)

Let this poem by Robert Frost get your mind open to—The Sound of Trees.

I wonder about the trees.
Why do we wish to bear
Forever the noise of these
More than another noise
So close to our dwelling place?
We suffer them by the day
Till we lose all measure of pace,
And fixity in our joys,
And acquire a listening air.
They are that that talks of going
But never gets away;
And that talks no less for knowing,
As it grows wiser and older,
That now it means to stay.
My feet tug at the floor
And my head sways to my shoulder
Sometimes when I watch trees sway,
From the window or the door.
I shall set forth for somewhere,
I shall make the reckless choice
Some day when they are in voice
And tossing so as to scare
The white clouds over them on.
I shall have less to say,
But I shall be gone.

Find a picture of a bare tree, or if it is winter look outside and turn off all the noise around you, and study the tree up and down. Or better yet how hungry are you for His presence to embrace you like a thick warm blanket freshly out of the dryer? Lets take a walk outside to the nearest forest of trees with no leaves. Bring a pen along and maybe your phone to record the noises. When you find a safe place to sit within the bare trees, close your eyes, let go of all your thoughts and listen. There is so much more going on around the creeks and moans of the cold trees. The leaves down below rustling all around, the tiny snaps of broken limbs, the wind in control of the movement all around work together in harmony.

When you open your eyes, do you see the trees in a new perspective?

Are you able to see yourself among the trees?

(Take a picture and tag me in it with hashtag #thepilgrimageofdivorce)

You will forget your misery; you will remember it as waters that have passed away. And your life will be brighter than the noonday; its darkness will be like the morning. And you will feel secure, because there is **hope***; you will look around and take your rest in security.* (Job 11:16-18)

> "Behold, God is my helper; the Lord is the upholder of my life." (Psalm 54:4) ESV

My hope does not come from what a relationship can bring me because my hope is the Lords desires He's placed in my heart. These are not some fantasized dreams but something God placed in my heart to prepare for. Someone coming behind me and holding me in the kitchen while I cook, snuggling close, and having deep conversation by a fire, listening to a thunderstorm and then running in the rain together, that touch, that quality time. The desires burn within, yes.

When the Lord becomes your confidence and hope your focus will not be infatuated with what you do not have, but what you do have. My faith and reliance on the Lord has never been so pure and real. **Worry is not part of my vocabulary any longer as I serve a God that is faithful and just**. He will take care of my desires. He will supply my every need. My desire is God Himself, not overabundant blessings, but Himself, my God.

My hope in the Lord has been found through admitting my helplessness.

Now it is time to love Him freely and let Him refresh you with His holy embrace.

RETURN TO HIS LOVE

"I know you are enduring patiently and bearing up for my name's sake, and you have not grown weary. But I have this against you, that you have abandoned the love you had at first." (Revelation 2:3-4 ESV)

I cry out to God—get me back to you—my first love. But, here I am crying out the same plea with revelation that I need not be here again. I desire more, I desire a deeper knowledge of God being my first love. When he studied me in the womb of my mother, He intricately knitted me, and made me perfect.

Psalm 139:13 says He *"formed our inward parts"* and I am seeing new light to this as my inward is my soul and emotions, where conflict with spirit and flesh take part. The emotional part of me has been made to be vulnerable, to give away pieces of me that were ultimately created for Gods pleasure, not mans. The world has distorted the word pleasure—do not take God as a pervert and wanting us as men drool at the mouths over a woman's body. God created us to enjoy His unconditional love, to give Him our hearts, for us to give Him our everything. THIS is the place He keeps bringing me back to. Give up earthly desire of man. Tune my senses into God—may I smell His sweet aroma, may I touch beauty He has created as a gift, open my eyes to your presence, awaken my soul so I hear your calling, and grace my lips of speech so they are pleasing to you.

"O woman, great is your faith! Be it done for you as you desire" (Matthew 15:28 ESV)

When I first read this, the focus became about me. And how much I do desire to be a woman of great faith. This is a great desire; but there is so much more to this that was revealed to me. This Gentile woman did not make this about herself, but humbly had faith to allow Jesus' healing ministry to operate.

Here is why this pierced me individually. As I have been running to earthly pleasure in man, even when God asked me gently to give Him a year of my devotion, and to write on my journey to reach many other women dealing with the same traps of giving our bodies and empty love to an earthly relationship. I realized often that I was being no different than the world. The desire I had to commit to Gods calling on my life was not changing me, it was not growing me, it was only opening more doors to darkness. So I thought. As O. C. said..."*turn away for one second out of obedience, and darkness and death are at work at once.*"

My disobedience and my lack of faith kept me from the light, and kept me from the blessings of Jesus wanting to use me for His healing ministry to many aching hearts of women. I postponed His calling everytime I chose my way over His ways.

O.C. also reminded me in his wisdom over one weekend— "Obey God in the thing He shows you, and instantly the next thing is opened up."

I don't know what God is wanting to show you, only you know deep down. When will we as women give our whole heart to the Lord and stop running to what our bodies want?

Obedience requires sacrifice.

And I know my sacrifice will be giving up the pleasures of being told I am beautiful by a man, cooked for, admired, that instant text if I want it…but what are these things compared to the steadfast love of the Lord. To the blessings He showers down on us each day. And to the constant pursuit of our hearts. Today I pray for my heart to be opened to these blessings as more than enough.

That I will take the plunge to *"cause my faith to continue to grow, O Lord"* (2 Cor. 10:15)

You are not alone in your struggle. You are not alone in wanting man over God. You are not alone in your disobedience. You are not alone in your tears. You are not alone in your confusion.

May you and I let the struggle become a stepping stone for Jesus' healing ministry in our life.

May you and I give our whole hearts to the Lord today. So we can taste true satisfaction that does not linger with guilt and shame.

May you and I obey to what God is calling us to do today.

May you and I pray for one another today as our tears are not meaningless.

May we remember that God is not of confusion, and when we are confused we cast it out in Jesus name as this is not of God.

God is clear with His commands, it is up to us today to obey and commit to spiritual growth.

I know there have been words thrown at you that cut you to your deepest core, but can I assure you that those words do not define you. *"You drive me crazy and I do not love you anymore"* These were words I held onto for too long. As I know I am just as guilty for throwing out rash words to my x as well; I wish I could go back and change. But, as I was driving one morning to go pick up my kids in the bitter cold—I was warmed by the words of Jesus....

I never stop loving you.
I never give up on you.
I am committed to you and never break my promises.

It brought tears to my eyes though when I heard God say... ***"I will never stop loving you."***

If you remember anything from this book, remember this....

God accepts us. He does not reject us.
God waits on us. He does not give up on us.
God pursues us. He does not leave us.
God heals our broken hearts. He does not put doubt in our minds.
God is faithful. He never lies.
God will always protect. He never will leave us for the wolves.

"I swear by myself, declares the Lord, that because you have done this...I will surely bless you." (Genesis 22:15-19)

    I had a wake up call one day when I realized my mind and heart were in conflict with trusting God but no joy was resounding. I trusted God in what He has asked of me but, there was a dull ache inside still. I asked myself one day, if I trust Him, I should be joyful, right? I should be excited of what is to come, right? However, this was not the case. I found myself irritable and not very joyful at all.
But I found myself encouraged by Abraham; when God told him to go-- he trusted God, but there is no word of him rejoicing when he and Isaac set out that morning. All that is written is the most important lesson of all—Abrahams prompt obedience. This was only a test from God; a very extreme test might I add. However, Abraham feared the Lord and did as he was told.
    The summer of 2014 there was no word when God told me to give Him a year of the end blessing and reward. **And today I may still not be rejoicing but I am awakened that too many times we focus on the blessing rather the goal of God alone**. *"At any cost, by any road means nothing self-chosen in the way God brings us to the goal."* Oswald Chambers. God knows I would not have chosen this road, as He was still working on me.

Where are you today?
Does this hit home with you?

Are you focusing more on the blessing or God alone?

Maybe the blessing is God alone, and not what we would choose for ourselves. I still need some chiseling to grasp that one, as I know what my heart desires on this earth. And this morning I was on my knees asking the Lord...but this is not the goal, nor the lesson God wants to teach me right now. But, I know He cares for our desires that run rampant in our hearts--never doubt that. But, I am certain He desires our full devotion to Him first.

"Keep thy heart with all diligence; for out of it are the issues of life." (Proverbs 4:23 KJV)

Snow is falling as I type, and I cannot help to be pulled into the contrast of it heavily falling but still so gently it is descends to the ground. Peace comes over me when I see the heavy but gentle heavenly sugar land.

Yesterday I turned 32. God came over me like this snowfall, heavy on point, but gentle with His direction. At 32 years of age He said, <u>your heart has been conditioned to the affection of man, why not let Me retrain your heart to be the normal</u>. Not what society says you need for fulfillment. This ache that resides in me has been conditioned to thinking it needs a man to fill it when "lonely". You know that ache we long for when we see a couple holding hands, smiling and laughing together, and admiring one another? Yea. I know you get it. Because if we do not see it first hand, we see it in movies, billboards, magazines, and social media. And there is definitely nothing wrong with desiring companionship, as God created us to "Be fruitful and multiply and fill the earth and subdue it" (Genesis 1:28) The issue comes when we find our heart and mind to be occupied with the love of man for satisfaction, and not seeking the One who created us to love.

I think it is obvious why in scripture we are told to "keep our heart with diligence." We are constantly being bombarded with distractions. Diligence takes concentration. Our heart is a muscle that needs daily strengthening, and I am to a point where I desire to have it revived by Gods love and affection. I envision God massaging my heart with His pierced hands, bringing back to consciousness—slowly waking it back up to the sweet reminder that He's the One that has been pumping life into me everyday.

What steps are you willing to take today to let God retrain your heart to His?

"Then Jesus was led up by the Spirit into the wilderness to be tempted by the devil." (Matthew 4:1 ESV)

Does God have your attention yet? This season of being alone is a treasure and we need to guard it with all our heart. We have been lead to this wilderness not by accident, but for a big purpose!

God does not ever owe us an explanation, but a revelation.

And this revelation of this pilgrimage makes my heart skip a beat with joy. And come on, by now you know I do not like being alone. I have rebelled so hard against it I have given into sexual temptation just to feel close and secure, BUT, this is not where God has lead me to. I only lead myself there, by my own choice. He has been trying to lead me away from this bondage of sexual sin. **And leading me out into a wilderness far, far away**, so far He even asked me to give Him a year of no man being in my life. Did I listened 100% of the time.....no....but, slowly and surely because of His steadfast love my heart was mended because of His pure pursuit. My eyes were opened and my scars came to the surface. Running to sex was an easy way out of not really engaging emotionally with another person. I now have to face all the images in my mind that haunt me from past sexual failures. But with them being there it only makes me that much more cautious and respectful of who I am in Christ. I have to fight them off with scripture. And will I still crave it, hell yes.

Some may say how can one be facing any pain if they were the one that caused the divorce? I wholeheartedly believe in genuine repentance, but it takes the other party to forgive and choose "for better or for worse." Even in my time of darkness, there was conviction and then loyalty to confess where I was wrong. When looking back I do not even recognize that person. We can only learn from our past and not let the chains of lies choke us from moving forward. Eventually one of the parties will choose to invite someone else into their lives even when the other may have much faithfulness left to give. And that may be you; but your commitment is to the Lord now. Listen and obey to what He is asking of you this day.

He is drawing you near. He is taking you somewhere way deeper than you ever could have imagined. Do you feel it? Have you embraced Him with arms open wide? This call out of desperation has nothing to do with our feelings and emotions, as they are as wishie washie as the waves come in and out at sea.

"We pray in response to God Himself"...as Timothy Keller puts it.

When you are weak, you pray for strength.
When you are ill from miserable depression, you pray for joy.
When you are down to your last penny, you ask Him to be your Provider.
When you are weeping, you ask for Him to hold you and be your Comforter.
When you are bitter, you ask the Lord to change your perspective.
When you are tired of feeling used and come see yourself as dirty rags, you ask the Lord to cleanse you, mend you, and bind up your wounds.
When you feel all alone, you ask for the Lord to make your home a dwelling place.
When you are seeking attention from the world, you ask the Lord to allure you and to speak tenderly to your soul.
When you do not have the words, you ask Him to be your mouthpiece.
When you are anxious, you beg for Him to be your confidence.
When you forget who you are you ask Him to be your Identity.
When you do not feel beautiful and desirable, you ask Him to take your hand, lead you to a place where the grass is so green His beauty outshines any person you are comparing yourself to.

I am beside myself right now as the Lord is revealing His pursuit to me once again.

We pray in response to His alluring.

He longs for us to be His everything. We may ask for the Lord to take away our pain, but I believe it goes way deeper. Begin writing down your prayers and see how the Lord is drawing you to Him.
Why would you be asking for Him to be your strength, comforter, provider, identity, mouthpiece, beauty, joy, mender, and lover? We ask because He is. We ask because He has made His name known. We ask because we were created in His image. We ask because we are responding to His pursuit.

We all long to be adored, admired, and just simply desired. We want to be swooned under the stars with soft music playing in the background. We want to be held so close and feel safe from enemies harm.
No matter how much we yearn for the love of a man that leads from the Lords direction;

JESUS WILL ALWAYS WANT YOU MOST.

His pursuit began with a song; that turned into a familiar rhythm; a constant beating that was so close it became our refuge. His pursuit began with protective walls that embraced us and kept us secure. **We long for what He has provided for us all along**. We long for what has been in our bloodstream, our touch, and our sound waves from when He spoke life into our mother's womb.
He never gave up on us. He never left us when we cried our first tears. He never stopped singing sweet melodies to our souls. He never stopped holding us close. He has been waiting for us to return to Him. He has been waiting for us to acknowledge His unfailing love. He has been calling us home.

He knows us from the inside out, backward and forward, every hair on our head, every scraped knee, all the tears we have shed are bottled up and not forgotten. He wants all of you.

> *My heart bursts its banks,*
> *spilling beauty and goodness.*
> *I pour it out in a poem to the king,*
> *shaping the river into words (Psalm 45:1) The MSG*

Do you ever find a scripture and it just makes your heart start singing? It comes so alive within you; you just cannot contain the beauty of vision the Lord is presenting before you? I imagine myself in the middle of a river where the vision turns into a painting. All I can see is my back, my hair down—hands are raised embracing and holding hands with the gentle breeze wrapping around me, coming in and out between my fingers. The current is gently brushing the skin of my legs, going in one direction—**forward**. It is calling me to follow it, but my eyes can only see so far as it curves like the letter S. And this letter S shapes before me the pilgrimage the Lord has carried me through in this past year. And this day I see in this vision all He is to me today. He has turned the storm into a calm peaceful river. And this vision came to life after much wandering and trying to be God. I am sure if looking from above and down at the paths I have taken would shape into the letter S. There was much going back and forth, but always going forward down the stream toward life. I was only moving forward due to the pursuit of His love. He was always saying, follow Me—it was only when I tried to go back up current I was in distress and turmoil. There was no peace when trying to go the opposite direction of His calling on my life. . **If there is conviction, peace will not expound**. It is only when we let Christ lead our hearts we will find peace. *"Let the peace of the Messiah, to which you were also called in one body, control your hearts. Be thankful." (Colossian 3:15)* Be thankful for His leading. Be thankful for His pursuit. Be thankful for His grace. Be thankful for Him never giving up on you. Be thankful

He is waiting for your return. Be thankful He is the giver of peace and not confusion. Rejoice.

This day I encountered a vision through the peace of The Spirit. He has poured out His goodness to me in poem and water. He knows how to swoon my heart, as poetry and the sound of water is where I find myself lost in His presence. Once I learned His pursuit for my heart was not to harm me but to love me I was able to let go of all the things of the world that were distracting me from His Presence. And over time as God always does-He lead me to a place where I am confident in these words He revealed to me.

Satisfied
Secure
Steadfast Love
Safe
Swelling in my heart
Songs of joy
Sword—Wisdom of the Knowledge of His Word
Still Water-- Peace

Sanctification— The beautiful thing is, He is still working on me and you even once we get to a beautiful place of freedom.
"There has never been the slightest doubt in my mind that the God who started this great work in you would keep at it and bring it to a flourishing finish on the very day Christ Jesus appears." (Philippians 1:6)

January 24, 2016

Today is a new day. A day where I can confidently say I am okay being alone at night. I rather be immersed in Gods Word than engaging in a conversation with man. I can confidently say remarriage may not be in the Lords will for me, and I am completely content in that. Jesus is enough. Jesus conquered the sin that tried to destroy me. Jesus has the most fierce pursuit which is rewarded with peace. Peace is a gift that He grants to us each day; it is up to us to reach out and grab it, trust it, and live with it.

THANKFUL HEART

I cannot end without sharing my grateful heart to the ones that stood by my side, took me in, listened to me, held me, encouraged me and pushed me to keep fighting the good fight. We all have a part to play in this life to carry friends and family along side of us to help get them back on their feet again.

A huge thank-you goes to my mom and dad, for they never judged me, they just loved me as best they knew how. My mom never missed a morning to text me and say good morning and then ask me later that day if I had eaten. My dads listening ear when I just needed to cry blossomed a beautiful relationship that I will forever cherish. And then the day my mom gave me some tough love that shook me to the core and lead me to the altar to lay down the entanglements I had with the world.

My best-friend that opened her home to me very early on when I couldn't sleep home alone. Stacy, thank-you for your southern hospitality, the way you love so fiercely, your beautiful smile that always lit me up on a gloomy day, and being my free-spirited friend that I have always needed.

My counselor, Jeff that gracefully did not give up on me, believed in me, prayed over me, and helped me regain my courage once again.

My iron friend, Pamela that sharpened me spiritually, prayed for me right when I asked her for strength, and our random middle of the night texts when we both could not sleep.

God orchestrated all of these relationships in His perfect timing to help get me where I am today.

Made in the USA
Lexington, KY
30 August 2016